THE REVENGE OF FRANKENSTEIN

BearManor Media
P.O. Box 1129
Duncan, OK 73534-1129

Phone: 580-252-3547
Fax: 814-690-1559
www.bearmanormedia.com

The Revenge of Frankenstein was
First published as a Panther Book - June, 1958
First BearManor Media Edition 2012
Revenge of Frankenstein produced by Hammer Films &
Released by Columbia Pictures, 1958

The Nightmares Series is being published to preserve original movie tie-in novels that were printed in the 1950s and 1960s on the old style pulp paper. We hope these reprints will allow them to last into the new century.

THE NIGHTMARE SERIES

Brides of Dracula by Dean Owen
Revenge of Frankenstein - Uncredited

THE REVENGE OF FRANKENSTEIN

Based on an original screenplay
by Jimmy Sangster
with additional dialogue by
Hurford Janes

Philip J Riley's

This volume is dedicated to
Jimmy Sangster
(2 December 1927 – 19 August 2011)

IF I Had a ......HAMMER!!!!
"THE REVENGE OF FRANKENSTEIN"
By Richard A. Ekstedt

The first time I had ever seen "Revenge Of Frankenstein" was NOT on the silver screen at the local theatre (The Lane in New Dorp or The Paramount in Stapleton, both located on Staten Island. NY) or the then VERY restricted medium called television. No.... It was in a basement, and it was in the 'wonderful' format called '8MM'. I knew a Hammer Film fanatic from Eltingville (again, Staten Island, NY), one town over from where I lived, who was a big collector of all things Hammer Films. The fellow's name was Douglas (who loved to talk in a overdone British accent), and he called me up, excited, that he had a silent 8mm COLOR copy of "Revenge Of Frankenstein" he had just got in and wanted to see if I was interested in viewing it? I was!!!!!

There was no sound as this was a silent copy with words printed on the film (there were sound projectors coming out at this time but the price was above most of our means-the reel..er..real goal was 16MM) but the visuals were great and it started getting me hooked on these British thrillers I have come to know and love.

Looking back to those times now, the very first time I saw a Hammer Frankenstein movie, in fact, on the big screen, was (the only Hammer so far I had seen were on the tube: "The Creeping Unknown"("The Quatermass Xperiment"), "X The Unknown" and "Spaceways") at the Lane Theatre, and it was, to my enjoyment, a Hammer Film double feature. The combo was "The Mummy's Shroud" and "Frankenstein Created Woman". For me, having watched the old B/W Universal movies on television, this was a wonderful new experience and it was getting better and better as I caught up on LOTS of lost time.

One of the things I discovered, of course, is that unlike the series of films put out by Universal Pictures, this was about the Creator (who, granted, at times, was a Monster himself!), Baron Victor Frankenstein and his search for knowledge. The Baron was obsessed in his quest, cold blood, and without a conscience-a 19th Century Josef Mengele- who saw human beings as fodder for the mill! This was a far cry from Colin Clive in the original 1931 "Frankenstein" (and sequel, "The Bride Of Frankenstein") who played the scientist filled with tormented guilt for what his creation wrought!

The series brought forth by Hammer Films started in 1957 with "The Curse Of Frankenstein" (which introduced in his first reel role as a monster, a fellow named Christopher Lee!) and was followed by "The Revenge Of Frankenstein" 1958, "Evil Of Frankenstein" 1964, "Frankenstein Created Woman" 1967, "Frankenstein Must Be Destroyed" 1969 and "Frankenstein And The Monster From Hell" 1971. These movies starred British television and cinema star, Peter Cushing (whom I personally met once, and engaged in a conservation with him in our mutual love of the comic duo, Laurel and Hardy). Mr. Cushing appeared in the classic "Chumps At Oxford" playing a student who conspires to play a prank on the comic team. There was a 1970 Hammer Film called, "The Horror Of Frankenstein"(a remake of the 1957 first in the series, done as a comedy with Ralph Bates as the Baron).

Peter Cushing , who had worked in Hollywood and appeared in "The Man In The Iron Mask" 1939, "Vigil In The Night" 1939 and "Howards Of Virginia" 1940 would later return to the U.K. to become a major British television star ("1984", "Richard of Bordeaux", "The Browning Version", "The Moment" and "The Creature"-which would be filmed by Hammer as "The Abominable Snowman Of The Himalayas" in 1957). While he had appeared in such motion pictures as "Hamlet", "Moulin Rouge" and "The Black Knight", it was his association with Hammer Films that led to worldwide recognition and a legion of fans.

Peter Cushing would continue to work in motion pictures until 1985, appearing in "Biggles-Adventures In Time". The final project he did was narrating "Flesh And Blood" (with old friend and co-star, Christopher Lee), an excellent documentary on Hammer Films produced by Ted Newsom.

The Revenge of Frankenstein

For me, "The Revenge Of Frankenstein", was the best of the Hammer Film Frankenstein series. Like James Whale before him, who started "Bride Of Frankenstein" where the 1931 classic left off, director Terence Fisher started "The Revenge Of Frankenstein" where its predecessor (1957s "The Curse Of Frankenstein") ended where Baron Frankenstein is being led to the guillotine for the murders his creation did. Instead, he escapes with the help of a deformed prison worker, Fritz (Oscar Quitak).

Changing his name to "Doctor Victor Stein", he relocates to the city of Carlsbruck where he begins fresh in new experiments. Having perfected his skills and having a willing subject in Fritz, who wants a normal body, the Baron is ready for transplanting a live human brain! By chance, another doctor named Hans Kleve (played to perfection by Francis Mathews), has recognized the Baron and begs to take himself on to learn from, whom he considers ,the greatest living mind of the day. The Baron, intrigued, agrees to this! Baron Frankenstein takes Hans to his new lab and shows the young doctor a normal looking body (Michael Gwynn) preserved in cold, that is to be Fritz's new host. The Baron tells his new assistant that the only thing that could go wrong is that if any trauma to the brain, while recovering, could result in violent dementia-including cannibalism!

With the Charity Hospital the Baron runs and its diseased, infected patients (supplying him with fresh material) all seems working to plan until a woman, Margaret (Eunice Gayson), daughter of a high political official, is forced upon the Baron and Hans. The chain of events she unwittingly puts into motion causes disaster for all!!

The film was a collection of excellent British acting talent. Besides Peter Cushing, you had in supporting roles, Eunice Gayson, who would later be known as 'Sylvia Trench' in the James Bond film version of "Dr. No" and sequel, "From Russia With Love"(with Sean Connery); Francis Matthews (best known to many as the voice of Captain Scarlet) and would appear in the sequel to the first Hammer Dracula film, "Dracula-Prince Of Darkness"(as well as in the Hammer "Rasputin The Mad Monk"(both starring Christopher Lee). Also, in supporting roles were Michael Ripper, Richard Wordsworth, Lionel Jeffries and Michael Gwynn, as the tormented 'creation', Karl.

Terence Fisher, showing his talent in previous Hammer Films, once again pulled it off, enhancing Jimmy Sangster's intelligent script (with additional dialogue by Huford James) and Jack Asher's incredibly moody photography. The film was released in the U.S. in June of 1958 with an August release for the U.K. that same year. "The Revenge Of Frankenstein" had enough positive feedback that Hammer Films projected more outings for the good Baron (especially after the events that concluded this story).

Hammer Films, as a ploy to get interest in this latest outing with Baron Frankenstein, elected to publish Jimmy Sangster's screenplay in paperback thru Panther Books (Richmond Hill Printing Works and published by Hamilton &Co. Ltd, London). I couldn't find a name on my edition of the film tie-in and can, right now (and until someone can report otherwise), only speculate that Jimmy Sangster himself wrote this at the request of Hammer Films.

The book follows the film rather closely and captures the somber tone of most of the movie. "The Revenge Of Frankenstein" novel received what appears three publications, reprinted in August and October of 1958. As far as I can tell, at this time, it has never been published in the United States but later, writer John Burke, issued a new variation of this story (told First Person by Baron Frankenstein himself) in a collection of published Hammer Film stories under the title, "The Hammer Film Omnibus", (Pan Books in 1966. Reprinted 1973) published in the U.K..

The credit to bringing this back into print, and for the first time in this country, must go to my Friend Philip J. Riley-noted cinema archeologist and dedicated writer of Cinema who has contributed his time and energy recovering such titles as "London After Midnight" and "A Blind Bargain" in book form. Thanks Phil! You're The Man!

For myself, in the role of grave robber ("There ya go, Matey! Lookin fresh as a daisy!"), it is a privilege to play a part in this book series!!!!

So sit back with a glass of wine, open the book to the imagined sound of the gong of funeral church bells and let the drama unfold!!!!

Richard A. Ekstedt
The Wilds of Pennsylvania
2011

Note: on August 19, 2011 JIMMY SANGSTER left us all at the age of 83. Born James Henry Kimmel Sangster, December 2, 1927, he became a driving force in Hammer Films as a writer and later, as a director (Hammer Films "Lust For A Vampire", "Horror Of Frankenstein"). He also wrote for U.S. television for such shows as "Kolchak The Night Stalker", "Ironside", "McCloud""The Six Million Dollar Man" and "Banacek", to name just a few.

Philip J. Riley and I would like to dedicate this book to his memory. This one's for you, Jimmy!!!!!!!!!

Jimmy Sangster

". . . and as the Baron Frankenstein has been adjudged responsible for the actions of the monster which he created . . . you are charged to carry out sentence of death by beheading. . "

So read the instructions on the warrant— but Frankenstein did not die!

This is the gruesome, horrific story of Frankenstein's revenge which took the form of an operation to remove the brain from one man, and transplant it in another. Karl, the unfortunate victim of the Baron's machinations, comes to a tragic end, tormented by his new-found freedom and, finally, destroyed by it.

This gripping drama has been filmed by Hammer Film Productions Ltd., and stars Peter Cushing, Eunice Gayson, Francis Matthews and Michael Gwynn.

Jimmy Sangster

PROLOGUE

THE gray turrets of the prison fingered into the morning mist. Below, the courtyard was empty save for the crude wooden platform which raised the guillotine from the uneven flag stones.

Alone on the scaffold, the executioner was winding the blade to the top of its frame. The rope creaked and the wheel squeaked as it turned. The knife came to a rest near the top.

At the foot of the guillotine there was a plain wooden coffin. The executioner opened it and placed the lid ready on the floor. Then he took from his belt the warrant for his morning's work and pinned it in its place of the uprights of the scaffold.

He was old in the work. In earlier days there would have been a crowd to watch him, and proudly he would have read out the instructions on the warrant before he carried through his grisly task.

He pulled his mask down over his face and spat in disgust; there was no longer any glory in this job. He smoothed the parchment down against the wood and squinting through the slits in his mask he clumsily spelled his way through the words.

. . . AND AS THE BARON FRANKENSTEIN HAS BEEN ADJUDGED RESPONSIBLE FOR THE ACTIONS OF THE MONSTER WHICH HE CREATED WHICH INCLUDE MURDER YOU ARE CHARGED BY THE COURT TO CARRY OUT ON THE BARON FRANKENSTEIN SENTENCE OF DEATH BY BEHEADING . . .

Baron Frankenstein. The man who had made a man. A man which had become a bloodseeking monster. A baron. This was no ordinary prisoner. The mouth under the mask twisted a little, but then this was to be no ordinary execution.

There was a heavy click and across the yard a door was closed. Away from it stepped the black-skirted figure of a priest. He settled his shovel hat on his head and there was a quick rustle of skirts as the priest walked to the scaffold.

The executioner shoved the end of the coffin clear of the steps.

The time was getting near.

As the priest reached the door it was flung back and out into the yard came three figures. The priest fumbled with the pages of his prayer book and stole a sideways glance at the prisoner and his guards.

Was this the man who had really discovered the secret of life? He said he had made a man, but it had been a monster. The priest looked; there was little to show of evil in the face of the man standing with his head held high.

There were little lines of superciliousness down the side of the fine aristocratic nose. The eyes were without expression.

The twisted figure of one of the guards pushed the prisoner forward. The priest could barely restrain a shudder. The guard was a stunted creature, a hunchback, but in his eyes there was fire. There was the look of a man of purpose.

The priest ranged himself in front of the prisoner and as the little procession was about to move across the yard the hunchback swung round and ordered the other guard back inside the prison. IT was as though he took an unholy joy in taking the responsibility for this man's death.

To the priest, this was one of the duties which his calling forced on him. He tried to keep his pace solemn and decorous though he would gladly have run.

"Hail, Mary, full of Grace . . . . Lord is with the . . . ."

Halfway across the yard.

"Blessed art thou amongst women and blessed is the fruit of thy womb. . ."

They began to climb the steps to the scaffold. Suddenly they stopped—there was a crash as the blade of the guillotine ran home. The executioner grinned evilly at his little joke.

Continuing his climb, the priest shook his head in disapproval. The prisoner with his arms tied behind him looked on coldly, and the little hunchback's fiery eyes caught those behind the mask of the executioner and they seemed to glory in an understanding.

Once more the executioner wound up the blade until it reached the top.

"Mother of God . . . pray for us now, . . . pray for us sinners in the hour of our death."

The blade was poised.

"Amen."

There was an unseemly little scuffle, a cry, and the blade crashed down onto the block.

To the outside world in 1860 so died Baron Frankenstein: scientist, doctor and maker of monsters.

"The Boar Tavern" was only a few minutes' walk from the outside of the prison. It didn't take long for gossip to move from the inside of the prison walls to the outside. After that it was only a short, quick and usually drunken step to "The Boar".

Most of the customers were only too well acquainted with what went on inside the prison walls. "

The Boar" was generally their first call after the gates had clanged behind them, and left them blinking in the unexpected light of freedom.

To the clients it was a place for a good strong wine, or a good strong wench. To the Town Marshal it was a "thieves' kitchen". Shrieks of bawdy laughter sounded through the smoke-filled bar.

One man turned his back on the bar and its hilarious bundle of people. He carried in his hands two large glasses of coarse red wine filled to the brim, the contents slopping down over his fingers.

He had a sly weasel face, and he carried the wine as though it were a tool to do his bidding, rather than a potion for a friend.

"There y'are, Kurt m'boy, what do you say?"

"I don't like it."

"What's wrong with it, Fritz—I just don't like the sound of it." Kurt's speech was thick and slurred and, having delivered this verdict, he took another deep swig of the wine.

It was Fritz—of the weasel face—who was the brain; Kurt was the brawn. It was clear to Fritz that he would have to try another tack. His mind scraped round for another approach.

"Look, my friend"—his boxy face assumed a hurt look—"You are my friend, aren't you?"

Kurt's big brow furrowed itself as he thought long and carefully, too long for the liking of Fritz; but in the end he agreed.

"Yes! I am your friend." The thought struck him as sentimental, and he gave a little sob as he sucked another mouthful of the wine.

"Well, since I am your friend, would I suggest anything that could go wrong?"

The answer was devastating.

"Yes," said Kurt into his glass. "I still got the sc-scars."

"Well,'ow was I to know they kept dogs inside the house?" Fritz renewed his attack.

"Look, Kurt, it isn't like that. We don't even have to break in anywhere." He looked around to see that no one was close enough to overhear. "—All we got to do is to go over to the churchyard an' dig it up, then take the body down to the medical school and I can get ten marks for it."

"You said six marks."

Fritz swallowed and looked uncomfortable; he fumbled for an answer.

"Well, I could get that if I bargain for it. I jes' didn't want you to be disappointed if we only got six."

Kurt subsided into his glass and ruminated.

"A'right, a'right, five for you and five for me,"

To give away five marks out of ten was breaking Fritz's heart but he had no choice. He looked at the ceiling in silent misery to think of some way to get himself a bigger share, but Kurt's wine-laden breath and bulging muscles drowned such hopes. Kurt jabbed him with a stubby forefinger.

"An' don't forget it's my spade."

Fritz knew he was beaten.

"All right . . . but," he clutched at his chest and coughed self-consciously. "I mustn't strain m' heart; you gotta do the digging."

Kurt patted him on the shoulder in agreement and the two men sat side by side saying little. The smoke was still thick in the bar room but as time passed the noise grew less, the bar emptied, and all that could be heard was the occasional cry from the upper rooms where the wenches were plying their trade.

The two body-snatchers sat waiting for the hour to strike when it was sufficiently sure that all good souls would be abed. They drank no more, now that the job was agreed.

The last wench retired upstairs, the landlord dragged the drunks into a corner to sleep it off til morning. He crossed to bar the door.

"Are you two going, or do you want to stay.

The landlord was accustomed to his clients remaining on a bench overnight. He was hard in the ways of the world. He encouraged them to stay. They could sleep on a bench for nothing, which meant that they could spend the money that they would have used for a room on wine and a loaf of bread in his bar.

Fritz had heard the church clock strike. It was late enough.

"No," he said, "we've got a place to go."

He roused Kurt, who had been dozing, and the two men hitched the coats round their shoulders and stepped out into the mist. Inside the bar they had been men relaxed. Outside they became tense; they were in the world of the righteous. The world of the God-fearing. The world of courts and judges and prisons . . . the enemy.

They slunk along close to the walls.

In the graveyard, a film of moisture rested on the tops of the tombstones. The new ones stood like a stunted grey forest of stubs, the old ones nodded intimately toward each other.

Their tools tucked under their arms, the two men were edging between the stones looking for one—the newest.

They stopped and picked out of the ground the crude wooden headpiece and the big man spat on his hands.

His spade struck into the ground with a metallic clink.

Later, from the trench he looked up at his companion sitting on the next headpiece saying:

"You've got to know where to look for these things. Take this one, for instance. He was only planted this morning . . . he'll be fresh as a daisy." He took another bite from the hulking meat sandwich clasped in his hands.

"Where's he from?" said Kurt from the trench.

"Who?"

The man Kurt thrust his spade into the earth of the grave.

"Him—this one . . ."

"Came from the prison this morning . . . . come on we ain't got all night."

The other sighed and started to wield his shovel in the grave again. In a little while his shovel struck shallow with a thud.

"This is it,"" he said and began scraping at the soil over the coffin. Gradually the crude pine box came into sight, and with his hands he cleared the last of the dirt away from the name plate on the lid of the box.

"Come and look at this."

He pointed down at the coffin lid. The other came over to his side and dropped down into the trench beside him.

The plate bore no dates—only a name.

"Baron Frankenstein."

"A baron! From inside the prison!"

"Come on, let's get him out and done with."

The two men set their hands to raising the meagre wooden box until they had managed to hoist it out onto the soil at the side of the opened grave.

They were now so near to their goal that they had lost their reluctance for the job.

With one of them steadying the box on the edge of the grave, the other pushed the blade of his shovel into the edge of the coffin lid. He levered bit by bit down one side.

With a screech of ripped nails the lid sprang upwards and was pushed quickly aside.

Eagerly the two men leaned forward and looked down into the coffin.

Their eagerness drained out of them and they slowly froze rigid in their attitudes. The sight in the coffin held them so that they could neither move away nor close their eyes and cease to look. Then the big one began to tremble as he looked down, and frantically he began to cross himself.

In the coffin, still in his robes, was the headless body of a priest. Resting on the chest was the wide-brimmed clerical hat in which he had crossed the execution yard that morning and . . . between his feet . . . between his feet was a round, badly wrapped bundle in sacking. The sacking was stained and speckled in blood.

For the one man, this was an end to the night's work.

He gabbled with fear, "It's a priest", and before there was time for another word, he scrabbled his way over the mound of dirt and fled into the night.

Automatically, the other was half-way to following him and then he paused. He set his foot back onto the fresh opened earth and looked down once more at the coffin.

"What if he is a priest?" he said softly to himself. "He is still a dead one. . . . Still worth ten marks to me."

He was rapidly gaining a hold on himself.

"The head's awkward . . . so you were a priest that went wrong, eh? Baron Frankenstein!" He bent down as though to pick up the head in its sacking from the coffin but gradually became aware that he was no longer alone by the grave.

His eyes travelled slowly from the coffin to the figure in the long grey cloak watching him from a few feet away. He looked into the cool face with the greying hair and at the straight, fastidious nose—the face of the prisoner who had crossed the execution yard that morning. The eyes caught the gaze of the body-snatcher and held his mind prisoner.

Even before the figure spoke, Fritz knew.

"Good evening," said the man in the tall straight cloak. "I am Baron Frankenstein."

Fritz turned to flee, but behind him, moving in unseen, was another figure. Short twisted, horrible, with eyes that burned like green fire.

For a moment he was caught between two minds, and then his brain whirled and whirled and his figure crashed dully into the bottom of the fresh opened grave.

The two figures made a step forward to reach him before he fell; they were too late.

Victor Frankenstein dropped into the grave by the body-snatchers side. The pulse was gone. He looked up at the twisted form of the hunchback and shook his head quietly.

Frankenstein and his hunchback replaced the lid on the coffin and bundled the box back into the grave. The shovels which had been used to exhume the unhappy priest were put to use for filling the grave.

Finally the hunchback patted the earth back to its prim little mound and Frankenstein stepped forward with the crude wooden head-piece.

For a moment he looked at the same on it . . . his own name. With a sardonic twist on his lips, he drove it into the soft soil.

Then, beckoning the hunchback, Baron Victor Frankenstein strode off into the night mist and a new life.

Jimmy Sangster

CHAPTER ONE

BARON FRANKENSTEIN decided on the city of Karlsbruck. It was large enough for him to set up a medical practice but sufficiently out of the way for there to be small risk of his running face to face with someone who had known him in his own land.

Once satisfied that the city would serve his purpose, he decided to risk one journey to his castle home.

Karl, the hunchback, and Frankenstein himself, had driven over the border, on a quiet track. As they neared Frankenstein's home they travelled only at night. Finally they scaled the last peak to the castle, on foot.

The night wind whipped at their cloaks as they crossed the portico in front of the iron-studded doors. But for the lights in the servant's quarters, the castle was deserted.

Frankenstein beckoned to the dwarf to follow him to a door half-hidden under some shrubs.

"Only the family have the keys of this door," murmured Frankenstein.

They walked along a narrow passage in the stone, and stepped out into the great hall.

They crept up the stairs past rooms, locked and covered in dust, until they reached the highest story; where there was a narrow staircase leading up to one room alone.

Frankenstein's laboratory.

The stairs creaked dully under their feet, and the dust from the wall clung to their fingers. Once more, from his pocket Frankenstein drew a key. The lock turned quietly.

Moonlight flowed coldly through the high glass roof. The rows of retorts were dusty, and the bench was littered with broken apparatus.

Victor Frankenstein turned to the hunchback.

"See, Karl, there it is; just as I told you."

As the two figures moved into the centre of the room, a rat scuffled from his place on a bench. Standing there, the two men were oddly contrasted. The one, thin and erect; the other, short, crooked, and shapeless.

Frankenstein counted the books, peering in the thin moonlight at the markings on the covers. He turned to the dwarf, who had been watching him.

"It is all there. I can make good my promise to you. It will not be quick and easy, Karl. You realize that? There will be many experiments before I will take the risk.

For the first time since he entered the house, the dwarf spoke. He shuffled over to Frankenstein and ran his finger lightly over the covers of the notebooks. It was his left hand; his right hand remained against his chest, a rigid paralysed claw.

"Frankenstein, I saved you from the scaffold. I kept my part of the bargain. Now it is for you to keep your part. You said you could give me a new body. I believe you. You *must* do it."

The little man's eyes glittered with the intensity of his feeling.

"Karl," said Frankenstein, "I promise that you shall stand as straight, and run as swift, as any man in the country."

The hunchback's eyes swept round the room.

"What more do we need from here?"

"Nothing. I have my books and that is enough."

The two of them slipped quietly out of the castle, and back over the border to Karlsbruck.

And so it was that the two of them screwed up a brass plate outside a door, and a certain "Dr. Stein" set up in practice.

Three years later in the City of Karlsbruck there was a time of warmth. The carriages clopped through the streets, footmen sat high and straight on the coach boxes. In front of them in the carriages the gay colours of the women's dresses and parasols made a pretty pattern of prosperity.

In 1863 Dr. Benz had not yet made his first motor car and the young bucks of the day would still make their morning bows from the backs of frisky gleaming chestnut cobs. Science was beginning to make a new prosperity which had yet to darken the city with smoke stacks, and pollute the rivers with its sewage. It could be said that in the year 1863 there was nothing but spring in the hearts of the inhabitants of Karlsbruck . . . that is, all excepting the hearts of the Medical Council.

The Medical Council was convening a cold and stormy session.

It was not often that the big Council room was put to its official use. Most of the time it served as a banqueting hall for the weddings of those whose houses were not of the size to accommodate the height and quantity of society that they wished.

Although there was nothing wrong with the individual finances of the members of the Medical Council, the Council as a whole was not averse to the income gained from the lease of its premises to those who were prepared to pay for it. That is, of course, those who were prepared to pay enough for it. After all, business was business and the port drunk by the doctors in the club room still had to be paid for.

But this day it was not a wedding party gathered at the long mahogany table. It was the Medical Council itself in full formal session.

The President of the Council shifted unhappily in his tall-backed chair at the head of the long table. The President was always unhappy when there was a Council meeting to be held. If it came to that, The President was always unhappy to be the President. It was not an honour he had sought. Somehow it was rather one that he had been unable to avoid.

Of course, he was one of the senior members of the medical profession in the district and that rather narrowed the choice to his group. The other and more distinguished of his colleagues had seemed to have so many adequate excuses ready as to why they should not be the President that he had found himself one day being congratulated and escorted a little dazedly to the chair at the head of the table.

The President sighed to himself. Out of the corner of his eye he could see that Molke was going to rise on his feet to speak. Molke was one of the worst. He was a bore, and he was pompous, and he always complained. He always seemed to create work, wanting to change the wine merchant, arguing about the bills for the lighting and the, of course, there was the unfortunate incident of the plumbing in the washroom. The President permitted himself an internal giggle; even if the Council had been made to foot the bill for a new suit, it had been funny. He tapped with his gavel—his feelings suitably hidden

"Yes, Dr. Molke, you may speak.

Molke was a large congested-looking man. After an insufferable long pause which was intended to heighten the effect of what he was going to say, he thundered on his stodgy way.

"I ask you, gentlemen, what do we know of this man, what do we really know about him . . .? What do any of us know?

He rocked back on to his heels and teetered there looking pleased with himself.

"This 'Doctor' Stein. He came here three years ago and set himself up in practice, without so much as a by your leave.

No one had ever heard of him before then. Where did he study?

"Where did he get his degree? What is his background, do any of you know."

He looked around the silent table,

"No. No more do I. And here he is, well established, the most popular doctor in Karlsbruck by all accounts . . . and he hasn't even applied for a place on the Medical Council. I have even heard it said that he says he can do without the Medical Council."

Molke leaned back, mapping himself after his exertion. The others at the table shuffled uncomfortably, knowing for once the accuracy of Molke's statements.

The President squinted unhappily round the table. This sort of speech was likely to cause a fuss; people would want him to do something. Bergmann was doodling on the blotter in front of him. Bergmann was a sharp one. Why couldn't they have made Bergmann President? He was always thinking of ideas. But Bergmann just doodled on and then without lifting his head he said:

"Looks as though he *can* do without the Medical Council, doesn't it? He has stolen half of my best patients."

"And mine," said young Kleve. There were other murmurs of assent from round the table. Molke pushed his silk handkerchief into it pocket.

"Exactly, and mine too."

"Your wife among them, I understand sir."

There was a ripple of laughter round the table and the President banged with his gravel.

"Gentlemen, gentlemen!" It was that young Kleve. The President tried to look imposing Clever fellow, that young Kleve, but he had no respect for his elders.

"I am sure Dr. Molke can look after his own family affairs."

Molke kept to his original point.

"The fact remains . . . this Doctor Stein must be made to join the Medical Council . . .or steps must be taken to see that he is no longer permitted to practise in this city."

Molke said down, conscious of having had his say to the full, for once, with the unanimous approval of his colleagues.

There was a pause. The President shifted uneasily in his chair. Of course it was Bergmann who put his finger on the problem. For a moment Bergmann ceased his doodling and raised his eyes straight to the still-perspiring Molke.

"Assuming he refuses to join, how do you intent to stop him from practising medicine?"

An uneasy silence descended over the table. Bergmann looked at Molke. The rest of them followed his glance and Molke sought refuge by looking to the President. Unfortunately for the President, there was no one left for him to look at. This was one of those moments he loathed. The moment when he was supposed to take the lead. He twisted the wooden gravel in his fingers. They were all looking at him and saying nothing, waiting for him to speak. He rose to his feet, if only to gain himself a little time. Yes, indeed, how could they stop the man from practising? The President cleared his throat.

"Hrrm, er, we have never, er, attempted to stop any doctor from practising in the city." They all looked stonily at him. He hastily changed his tack. However the refusal of Dr. Stein to join . . . er . . . to become one of us is an affront . . . er, yes, an affront."

This had a better reception, there was a warm murmur of agreement round the table. The President's fingers fluttered over his cravat and he clutched at a proverbial straw:

"Now . . . er . . . if there are any suggestions?

He beamed round hopefully. There were none. He beamed even more hopefully. With luck this was going to be one of those things which would quietly be shelved and eventually forgotten. He wouldn't have to do anything after all. He opened his mouth to speak.

"Oh well, in that case, er . . ."

His hopes were dashed by Bergmann. "Send a delegation to see him." It would be Bergmann of course.

The President twittered.

"Er . . . excellent, a delegation . . .made up of ?" he looked hopefully.

"Three," said Bergmann.

"Of course, three," echoed the President. "Three doctors here from the Council. Yes, that is what I suggest."

"Seconded," said Bergmann.

"All in favour?" said the President.

There was a chorus of agreement from the men at the table. The President himself beamed, this was going to be easier than he had hoped. He shuffled with his papers.

"Fine, fine; and now we come to the next item, er... the, er... city drains."

"Which of us goes?" It was Bergmann again.

"Huh?"

"Who makes up the delegation?"

The President fumbled in his mind, then had an inspiration as he caught sight of Molke.

"Oh Molke, of course." Molke nodded his acceptance. The President swallowed. Bergmann was the cause of this.

"Er, you, Bergmann?"

"No. I leave for Berne in the morning."

"Any volunteers?"

There were none. The President hopefully and then Bergmann nailed the lid on the President's coffin.

"I move that the President should go."

"Seconded," said Molke. The President squirmed unhappily. His wife would complain again and that would give him indigestion. He would do almost anything rather than have his wife complain, but his mind remained blank of excuses.

"Oh . . . er . . . if that's what you wish. Doctors Molke, Kleve and I will go and see this Dr. Stein." A voice from the end of the table said, "You had better make an appointment."

"He's right," said Bergmann. "His day is so dam' full you will never get to see him otherwise.

For the first time that afternoon the President managed to sum up a small genuine feeling of effrontery. "Fancy that! The President of the Medical Council having to make an appointment to see another doctor!"

There was no doubt about it, in three years Dr. Stein had made something more than an impression in Karlsbruck.

The "best people" had taken him up and a constant stream of the well-to-do flowed in and out of the surgery at the big old-fashioned house. It was not without reason that he had become such a favourite. It was not that he happened to have a good bedside manner. At times, as a matter of fact, one could say that he had become the most fashionable doctor in Karlsbruck in spite of his manner rather than because of it.

He was always courtesy itself but sometimes his eyes seemed to regard the object of their investigation with a detached, even contemptuous look. He was brusque when he felt he was wasting time; but one could not avoid the fact that he was the best doctor in the town. His cures had been remarkable.

He divided his time regularly between the well-to-do fee-payers and the ill-favoured charity cases. When tea cups were balanced in drawing rooms and gossip was flooding along, it was said the Dr. Stein was indeed a little peculiar in the amount of time he would insist on spending in his charity wards, and it was not that the charity wards regarded him as a ministering angel. That same coldness of eye and ruthlessness of decision made his presence more feared than revered. Yes, Dr. Stein was just a little odd, perhaps even a little frightening.

But this did nothing to alter the fact that in addition to being the best doctor in town, seemingly rich, and likely to become richer, he was handsome and unmarried. Dr. Stein was one of the most eligible bachelors in Karlsbruck and, as such, he suffered under a shower of well-to-do young ladies who were anxiously being pushed at matrimony by proud Mamas with an eye to securing their comfort in their own declining years. In the host of pushing Mamas, well to the front, was the Countess Barcynska.

It was a sunny afternoon, as the Countess billowed her way into the crowded waiting room, with her daughter trailing behind her rather like a dinghy being tossed by a barge.

As usual the room was crowded, crowded to the point of there being a shortage of chairs. The Countess was a woman of much determination and comparatively little scruples. She regarded such a situation as a little test for her ingenuity. She bore down on the weakest looking of the waiting room's occupants and confronted them with the statement:

"My daughter is liable to faint."

The two unhappy girls whom she addressed faded meekly from their places and having installed her Vera in place the Countess spread her own ample form on the other vacated chair.

Such an entrance was not likely to go unnoticed and a buzz of disapproval rumbled round the room. In the corner of the room stood a parrot cage with a large green parrot which every now and then emitted a saucous squak. All eyes were directed to the Countess and all tongues were clearly discussing her. The Countess was in no way put out and she fired a broadside in return. As the talk came to a tiny pause she boomed out:

"That poor bird." She swivelled her glance to the other occupants of the waiting room. "So much competition!"

The Countess was renowned for her tongue and though they might have expected such an attack, there were still eyeglasses raised in disapproval, which, for all the Countess cared, could have been directed into outer space. Poor Vera was not quite so thick skinned, and she let out a little "oh".

Her mother seized on it: "Ah dizzy again; the Doctor may insist you are cured, but I know better."

"I could have come by myself, Mama."

Countess Barcynska bristled. "What, and have you fainting all over the front step like a servant? Never!" She glared around the room. "How the doctor can find time to look at all these". . . there was an ominous pause, "ladies, and still find time to spend so much time in that miserable hospital of his. . ."

"He's very good to the poor, Mama."

"Fiddle-sticks! I hear he used them for research and experiments. I suppose that underneath all that grime and dirt the poor are the same as we are," she smoothed her ample skirt, "though I shudder to think so."

The doctor's consulting room opened, and another Mama and her daughter were escorted out.

The Countess rose to her feet.

"Come, Vera."

The Countess pushed her daughter ahead. "I'm sure everyone will understand your need, my dear." Everyone did understand only too well and they still considered the Countess the worst-mannered woman in the country.

The steel-blue eyes and the quiet incisive voice seemed to give a hidden meaning to Dr. Stein's ordinary request of "Next, please."

Frankenstein closed the door behind the Duchess, a professional smile fixed on his face. His mind rippled on. What a bore; it was this need for money. These eternal mothers and the simpering little daughters with their sweet-smelling flesh. Ah, well! At least this one was pretty.

Her mother was pushing her behind the screen to undress and prattling on:

"You must revise your diagnosis, Doctor, you must overhaul her."

Frankenstein pulled a drawer out of a mahogany chest and thumbed his way through the card index.

"Now let me see; what was your daughter's original complaint?"

"Really. Doctor Stein, how could you forget?"

Inwardly, Frankenstein raised his eyes to heaven, these mothers; outwardly, he tactfully murmured:

"She is not my only patient, you know, Countess," he patted the cabinet, "that is why I need to keep this index."

He glanced at the girl's card and came round the side of the desk. "We doctors are not magicians, you know. We cannot diagnose maladies which we do not think are there. I doubt if I can do much for your daughter."

The Countess gathered herself into a velvet- and fur-covered mountain and remarked rather pointedly:

"You are a man, doctor. You could do a great deal for her. Yes, you should come and meet my little Vera away from this work-a-day place. Now, soon, I am having a musical evening, perhaps?"

"Much as I like music, my dear Countess, I have very little time. A doctor is always on call."

The meek voice of Vera floated from behind the screen.

"I am ready, Doctor."

"So am I, Miss Vera," sighed Frankenstein, "you may come out."

The girl slid shyly round the edge of the screen, the thin silk shift she was wearing doing little to hide her body from his gaze. Oddly enough, without her clothes the girl seemed more sure of herself than when she was dressed. Perhaps she was aware of the magnetism of her body, of the rose-tinted nipples pouting against the thin transparent silk. Frankenstein was attracted, almost in spite of himself. He pulled himself together and solemnly applied his stethoscope to her breast. She pouted a little at him.

"That thing is cold, Doctor—the last time you used your ear."

Frankenstein sighed and put away his stethoscope and bent his head to listen to the warm beat of the heart beneath the shift.

There was nothing for him to do, not that he had expected it. He made a perfunctory examination—the girl was as strong as a horse.

He retired behind his desk and wrote out a harmless prescription and told the girl to dress. He knew that he would have to repeat this process throughout the afternoon with small variations. There would be other mothers and other girls, though not all as attractive as this one. He ushered the Countess and her fledgling out, and for a moment he sat musing behind his desk.

Eventually he would be free to go to the hospital. At least the people there were really ill. And then after that . . after that there would be his real work. The laboratory where he would make his dream come true. The work for which he put up with society and its imaginary ailments and the hospital with its smelly scrofulous beggars. The former provided him with money and the latter with—a little smile flickered grimly round his eyes—well, how should he put it? The other supplied him with, say . . . raw material.

The afternoon passed before he was able to take his cab to the charity hospital and change his expensive suit for the more workman-like khaki overall which he wore round its wards.

The surgery was small and dingy. There was a reek of disinfectant and ether which mixed with the smell coming from the coarse enamel bucket half-filled with bloodstained swabs and the other residue of his work. By the big roll-topped desk there was only one wooden chair. On his desk close to hand lay the coarse workman-like tools he needed. A wooden foetal stethoscope, a couple of thermometers in antiseptic fluid, a tray of cotton wool swabs and an open case of instruments.

Seeming oblivious of the smell and squalor of his surroundings, Frankenstein was a man working in his element. He was wiping clean a scalpel used on the last patient and bellowing to the waiting queue in the passage:

"Next!"

A pallid bedraggled young woman scuttled in, and the wooden chair creaked and rocked a little as she seated herself in it. Given other times and another place she might once have been pretty, but her pinched face was surmounted by hair matted with blood, and she seemed to know the routine.

"Afternoon, Doctor," she said.

Frankenstein slid the instrument he was cleaning back in its case and turned to her. For a moment he looked at her dispassionately and then a little recognition appeared on his face. He leaned over her and looked at her damaged head.

"Oh, Inga, not again! I thought your husband was still in prison."

"They let him out for good behaviour."

"Why didn't you tell him what I told you?"

"Oh, I did. I said I wouldn't have anything more to do with him."

"And?"

"Well, when he got up in the morning he hit me with a bottle."

Frankenstein's eyebrows went up quizzically.

"He can't help it, he loves me, Doctor."

Frankenstein turned away to hide his smile. It was quite hopeless.

"Well, let's tidy you up a bit," he said and set about working on the torn scalp. He as carefully stitching his way when the up-patient, Slensky, put his head round the door: He was a lean man and sly, and had become a sort of self-appointed factotum running errands round the little ill-staffed hospital. To Frankenstein he was a useful commodity, for he had a rare condition which Frankenstein was holding in check and studying at the same time. Slensky would never get better, but he never got worse, and he had long since realized he was on to a good thing which gave him a roof over his head and enough to eat with far less trouble than he had to obtain it in the world outside. He guarded Frankenstein zealously.

"There's three men to see you Doctor Stein . . . from the Medical Council."

Frankenstein paused in his work. He had long since been expecting such a visit. Pompous, ignorant, idiots, soft from fleecing well-to-do hypochondriacs. The sort of men who had hounded him from his work before. He had been a success as a doctor in this town and he would now have to cope with the inevitable professional jealousy. Small men with small minds, they irritated him.

"I can't see them now," he said "they'll have to wait till after surgery."

"They seem impatient, Doctor."

"I'll see them when I have finished." An imp of humour stirred in him, he would remind them what real doctoring was about. "Tell them to wait in the ward." Slensky was a little surprised at this. Even he, who was no lover of cleanliness, spent no more time in the odiferous precincts of the ward than he could help.

"In the ward?" he said agape, for these were gentry. Men with clean white linen, top hats and gold watch chains.

Frankenstein straightened up from his task and turned.

"The ward," he said coldly. "I said . . . the ward."

The up-patient scuttled his way out of the surgery out of range of Frankenstein's glare and made his way down to the lobby. He crossed in front of the three doctors and held open the door to the ward:

"If you gentlemen will come this way?"

They followed him through the door into the ward and he let the door wing shut. With an oleaginous sweep of his arm he indicated the close-packed beds filled with reeking, groaning humanity.

"The Doctor says for you to wait in here."

For a moment, the delegation as a whole was speechless, and it was Molke who exploded.

"This is intolerable."

The President of the Medical Council whipped out his handkerchief and thanked heaven his wife made a point of storing his linen in the fragrant smell of lavender. He held the handkerchief tightly over his nose and murmured:

"You must remember, gentlemen, these are the poor."

Inwardly he thought to himself how anyone could be cured in such surroundings he would never know; the stench alone would kill him.

Hans Kleve, the youngest of the delegation, was not so far detached from the memory of the similar charity wards in the teaching hospitals where he had taken his degree. He wrinkled his nose. The place stank, but at least there were some interesting looking cases. Nobody could say that Dr. Stein did not work for his money. Even as he was looking round the ward a hush fell on the place. He turned and looked to the far end of the room and the cause of the silence was standing in the doorway. As Hans looked so, in his mind, there was the stirring of a memory.

Frankenstein stood in the doorway and with some satisfaction surveyed the scene. The close-packed beds with hardly room for a man to squeeze between the. A room packed with material for study, a veritable gold-mine of flesh, and those three pompous asses from the Medical Council were standing there with their handkershiefs to their noses not realizing that here was his supply, anyone's supposed supply, of the material for knowledge.

Frankenstein moved slowly down the rows of beds, his mind only half on the patients. He summed up the delegation. The short one, hiding behind the silk handkerchief, that would be the President. He knew him by sight, a mediocre, ineffectual man. The fat one, if he remembered rightly, would be Molke; he had a lot of patients who had come to him saying Dr. Molke couldn't do anything for them. The third one, the young one, who was he? And why should the young one stare so hard in his direction?

Frankenstein deliberately and methodically began his round of the ward. He called over the only assistant in the ward, Gunther, a big thick-set male nurse, a one-time fighter, whose muscles were at times useful when patients were obstreperous.

The silent atmosphere was becoming so tense that Slensky the up-patient, could no longer stand it. He coughed and cleared his throat nervously and gesturing jerkily to include the whole ward, he blurted:

"That's Dr. Stein, gentlemen, seein' to the poor an' needy."

But the attitude of the "Poor an' needy" was not somehow the attitude which one would expect for them to have for a benefactor. At the best there was grudging respect for Frankenstein as he moved from one bed to the next. But here and there, the look that burned in the eyes of the men in the beds was little short of a badly hidden hate.

Frankenstein worked his way to where the delegation from the Medical Council was standing and at one of the beds he stopped with what seemed an extra interest. The patient had the upper part of his arm bandaged. The part which projected below the bandage was covered with an intricate tattoo.

Frankenstein lifted the arm and moved it slowly from side to side as he looked at the tattoo. Then seeming for the first time to acknowledge the presence of the delegation he pointed to the tattoo.

"Look at this . . . interesting isn't it?" He twisted the arm a little so that the full pattern showed.

"Quite a work of art, don't you think, gentlemen?"

The President shuffled uncomfortably. "Why, it's er. . ." He fumbled for a suitable non-committal reply.

"Very picturesque."

It was young Kleve who broke in. Why was it, thought Frankenstein, this Kleve should have such a different look about him? The other two were intruders and they acted with embarrassment but this young Kleve seemed to have an assurance which indicated that he had within himself come to terms with some problem and was confident in the answer. Frankenstein fingered the arm gently. It was a fine arm in many ways, with well-developed supple muscles and sensitive fingers. He looked into the patient's eyes.

"You'll have to have it off," he said brutally.

"'Ave what off?" the patient paled.

"The arm, man, it's no use to you."

"It doesn't hurt me now."

Frankenstein made to rise. "If you would rather die . . It's up to you."

"But, Doctor . . . I won't be able to work any more."

Frankenstein turned to the male nurse by his side.

"What is his trade?"

"He's a pick-pocket, Doctor."

Frankenstein looked back at the patient, who avoided his eye.

"Well, you'll have to find another trade, or use your other hand." He spoke to the nurse. "I will do it at five o'clock."

Frankenstein wiped his hands on a towel and addressed himself to the President.

"Amazing how dirty these people get. Keeps them warm, they tell me. . . . What can I do for you?"

The President cleared his throat, his finger twittered round the head of his cane:

"I am the President of the Medical Council. . . ."

"Congratulations," murmured Frankenstein and busied himself swabbing clean a patch of skin on the tattooed arm. Having done this, he took a hypodermic from the tray and examined it intently, completely ignoring the delegation. Oh heavens, thought the President, now perspiring profusely, the man was going to be awkward, but now they were here there was no alternative but to see it through.

"At our last meeting, hrrrm," he cleared his throat, "it was decided that you should become a member."

Frankenstein meticulously squeezed the air bubbles from the hypodermic.

"Really?"

The President prematurely felt relief flooding into him.

"Then you accept?" he asked hopefully.

Frankenstein with his needle now ready, leaned forward and deftly made an injection into the arm of the tattooed man. He withdrew the empty needle and dabbed the spot where he had made the injection.

"No," he said.

The President looked aghast.

Frankenstein stood up, wiping his hands fastidiously on a towel handed to him by the nurse. He stepped out from between the beds, the better to face these three men who represented the profession which had scorned his work and hounded him out of his home.

"When I arrived in Karlsbruck three years ago and attempted to set up practice," he said to them, "I was met by considerable resistance from the Medical Council, which apparently exists for the purpose of eliminating competition. I was, therefore, forced to build up my practice alone and unaided. Having grown accustomed to working alone, I find I prefer it. . . . Do I make myself clear, gentlemen?"

The President of the Medical Council and Dr. Molke looked momentarily speechless, one aghast, the other choking with fury. It was young Kleve who answered:

"Yes, you make it quite clear, Dr. Stein."

Molke could no longer contain his wrath.

"Stein! Do you think that you can just walk into a town and steal the patients out of other doctors' surgeries with lies?" He was bellowing at the top of his voice.

Frankenstein looked coolly round the stinking riff-raff of the charity ward.

"I didn't realize that these were some of your paying patients, Dr. Molke; but in any event, I feel that etiquette and the welfare of my patients demands that you should lower your voice. It has a very upsetting quality."

The President shifted uncomfortably and darted a quick glance at the occupants of the ward, who were clearly drinking in every word of the affair. If Molke shouted their business all round the ward, the patients would shout it all round the town, and that would not do at all. He pleaded:

"Molke, please, not in front of the patients."

Molke choked and continued in a strangled undertone. He thrust his round red face belligerently at Frankenstein.

"Stein, you have deliberately stealing my patients by treating them for illnesses which they did not have, by playing up to them. It's, it's" he choked over his words, "unethical, unethical conduct.

"Really, Doctor Molke," said Frankenstein, regarding him coldly. "I cannot be responsible for your failures in diagnosis. I do not see that it is unethical to correct them, if the patients come to me. It would seem to me that it is far more unethical to continue treating them without result when a second opinion might assist in their cure"

"Do you have the audacity to come touting for second-hand business from my practice, Stein? Because I can assure you, you won't get it."

"My dear Dr. Molke, it is Dr. Molke that I am addressing, isn't it? If your failures continue to clutter up my consulting room, I shall have to employ an assistant to deal with them alone in order that I can concentrate myself to the serious cases."

"Gentlemen, gentlemen, please." The President was hopping agitated on the tips of his toes. Things were beginning to get out of hand. "We are members of a highly respected profession, we cannot air our, er, differences like this in public."

Frankenstein acknowledged the President.

"Gentlemen," he said, "There is really very little purpose in our talking either here or anywhere else. I have put to you my point of view and I don't intend to alter it." He turned to the nurse, who was still standing by with the tray of instruments in his hands. "Have that fellow with the arm ready for me, will you, Gunther?"

"Good afternoon, gentlemen." He bowed coldly at the delegation and made his way between the beds toward the operating theatre.

Frankenstein was quietly elated. It was not a big victory, but it was a victory. They had been forced to come to him, not he to them. When his work, his real work, was completed they would come to him on bended knees to seek his aid and his knowledge. It did not bother him in the least to hear Molke's voice shouting after him.

"Stein! You haven't heard the last of this!"

CHAPTER TWO

THE man with the tattooed arm had gone under the anæsthetic struggling and swearing. Now he lay limp, breathing deep unnatural breaths. It was not a long job but it was a job over which the male nurse noticed the Frankenstein seemed to take even more than his usual care.

There had been the usual mess. The spurt of blood, that grating of the saw on bones, and Frankenstein's so careful treatment of the severed ends of the arm. To Gunther as he stood by handing over the instruments, it often appeared that the Doctor took more care of the pieces he removed than of the patient from which he removed them. But then who was he to criticize? The patients always got better, well a reasonable number of them did, which was more than could be said for some of the doctors he had worked for in Karlsbruck.

Frankenstein placed the severed arm carefully on a piece of cloth lying ready on the trolley. He folded the cloth round it.

"Well, he won't be picking any more pockets with that arm."

He wrapped the cloth around the arm. taking no notice of the patient, whose breath was wheezing stertorously. Frankenstein indicated the bundle in the cloth, which was now beginning to stain dull red at one end.

"There will be a messenger to collect this."

Gunther nodded. He was familiar with this particular messenger, and Gunther had noticed that every time the messenger had come, there had always been great care used by Sr. Stein to see that the operation was done so that nothing was damaged.

The messenger rarely appeared before dusk and small wonder. He was a dwarf and a hunchback. His right side twisted in paralysis.

Gunther was big, he was honest, and he was mainly muscle. He was accustomed to the messy business if illness and to death in its various forms. Yet he could rare watch the avid way in which the hunchback would pick up the parcels of specimens without a feeling of revulsion at this travesty of a human being.

This ugly little man would appear, and take away these parcels of flesh as though they were to him the most precious things on earth. Gunther ceased to speculate.

"Will you need me after I have got this fellow back into his bed?

"No, Gunther, that will be all."

"Very good, Doctor. I have arranged for your supper to be in the office."

The two of them lifted the inert figure off the table on to the trolley. Frankenstein watched as the nurse shouldered open the doors of the cramped theatre and dragged the trolley away down the corridor to the ward.

He straightened up and became aware that the muscles of his back were arching from the time he had spent leaning over the operating table removing the arm. He massaged the muscles with his hands and walked over to where the arm lay waiting for Karl, the hunchback, to come and collect it. Idly he turned back the flap of cloth. Yes, it was a good arm, a usable arm. Later that evening he would see just what use could be made of it.

Frankenstein swung his arm and his torso to loosen the muscles and made his way into his private office. In the meantime—supper.

He took off his bloodstained khaki overall and hung it up. Why on earth did patients worry so much about that overall? After all, it was only blood, and what was blood? Yes, what was blood? It was far more complex than he had originally thought. His mind roamed around the idea and automatically he ran through the motions of turning on the tap in the little hand basin, rolling up his sleeves, and washing his hands. He returned to the present when he had to find the towel. Where was the towel? They never seemed to put it in the same place twice.

He dried himself, rolled down his sleeves and slipped into his coat. In the greenish reflection that looked back at him he approved of the coat. He didn't particularly care for dressing up, but if he had to do it he liked to do it well.

His toilet finished, he seated himself at the big knee-hole desk.

As usual, on it was a tray. He always ate at the office it saved him a double journey from the house to the laboratory.

Frankenstein lifted the napkin from the tray and revealed a small roast chicken. He gate it an exploratory prod with a fork. It was good. He set about carving for himself. His long fingers grasped the pointed carving knife and delicately guided the blade along the flesh. In truth he didn't so much carve the chicken as operate on it.

Frankenstein was lifting the slices to his plate, and it needed every ounce of his self-control not to alter the smooth travel of his hand when the voice called to him out of the darkness where the oil lamp failed to cast its glow.

"A very fine piece of dissection, Dr. Stein."

Frankenstein turned sharply. Dimly he could see the figure seated in the dark corner. It rose out of the chair and moved idly toward him, the face still in the shadow, and only the long legs and the hand swinging the ebony stick visible in the pool of lamplight.

"You must forgive this intrusion, Doctor."

Frankenstein peered into the dark.

"So long as you realize it is an intrusion," he said coldly. The figure reached the table and Frankenstein looked up. It was Kleve, the youngest of the three doctors who had called on him that afternoon. The known is never as frightening as the unknown. Frankenstein relaxed, and began munching some of the chicken.

Kleve stood by the side of the desk, the black ebony stick swinging barely perceptibly.

"I felt I ought to come and have another look at you. After a few moments with you this afternoon I was certain I had seen you before."

Frankenstein paused for a moment in his meal.

"That is hardly surprising," he said. "I have been practising in Karlsbruck for three years now."

There was a little pause and Kleve continued, "I mean before Karlsbruck; a little more than three years ago at the village of Ingstadt. . . ."

So that was it; he had been recognized. Admit nothing. What was it the fellow wanted? Kleve's voice continued.

"I was attending the funeral of a Professor Bernstein. I was a last-year student at the University where the Professor was lecturing when he died."

So he had known Bernstein; that was all so far.

"The Professor was buried in the vault of a . . ."

There was no mistaking the inference of the pause.

". . . a Baron Frankenstein."

Frankenstein put down his fork. He really knew, but what did he want. If he had wanted to expose him, he could have gone straight to the judiciary, and they would have been humming round the place like wasps round a piece of meat. Frankenstein's hand held on to the razor-sharp carving knife.

"Am I the first to recognize you?"

Admit nothing, Frankenstein; put out a feeler.

"I gather your practice, like Dr. Molke's has also been suffering of late. Are you in need of money?"

The stick stopped swinging and the voice changed its timbre.

"I am in need of knowledge."

"Ha! if only the other members of the Medical Council had the courage to admit this."

Kleve stamped his stick down on to the floor and leaned his face down to Frankenstein's.

"I want to learn." The palm of his hand beat on the leather top of the desk. "I want to learn more than any University could ever teach me. I want to become a pupil of the finest medical brain in Karlsbruck, the finest medical brain in the world . . . you . . .*Baron Frankenstein.*"

Frankenstein played for a little time. The young man seemed sincere in this search for knowledge, and it was one thing which he, Frankenstein, could understand.

"If I refuse?"

"You won't refuse."

"Either way we look at it, it is blackmail . . . isn't it?"

"If my quest for knowledge strikes you as blackmail . . . then it's blackmail. I see it as an agreement for our mutual benefit. Your knowledge in return for my assistance . . . and silence."

So this was it. Frankenstein walked across the room and turned to study the young man. It was blackmail, in a way, but it was a much safer blackmail than money. There was something in the urgency of the young man's voice that gave a ring of honesty. A pupil, an assistant. Frankenstein scrutinized the young man. The fellow was no fool, he could learn and he could be useful, take a lot of the load of routine work from his shoulders; work that did not require creative thought but only painstaking accuracy. Then again, if he stayed, he too would be committed. Frankenstein tapped his teeth with his finger; it might be wise.

"I'm not an easy man to work with," he said.

"Few men of distinction are."

". . .and then how can I be sure that when you have absorbed as much knowledge as you seek, you will not give me away?"

"There is no way. But then, by the same token there is always a chance that at a future date you might consider eliminating any threat to your identity."

The young man was right. Now that the gauntlet had been thrown down it was all or nothing for both of them.

Frankenstein's smile flickered over his face. The fellow had nerve; he was almost beginning to like him.

"Well then, we shall both have to keep on our toes, shan't we?"

"Then you accept me?"

Frankenstein nodded.

"Yes, Doctor—er . . ."

"Kleve . . . Hans Kleve." The other bowed.

"There is just one thing. Tell me, are you squeamish, Doctor Kleve?"

The young man's face assumed an expression of quizzical humour.

"It is a poor doctor who is squeamish," he said.

Frankenstein surveyed him. "True, but the nature of some of my experiments is a little unusual."

"Try me," said Kleve.

"I will," said Frankenstein, nodding slowly and extending his hand. "I will."

The tenseness in the room lessened the moment the two men shook hands on their bargain. Kleve flung his cape back from his shoulders.

"Well? When do we start?"

Frankenstein fell in with his mood.

"There is no time like the present, is there?" He reached to the hook for his hat and cape. "Incidentally, you will promise to exercise great caution when you address me . . .the name is Stein . . . Victor Stein. My other official self is dead and buried,"

They moved to the door and Hans Kleve held it open.

"Allow me . . . Doctor Stein," and he bowed the other out into the passage with a good humour.

Outside the night air was chilling and the two men wrapped their cloaks round themselves. Frankenstein unhitched the reins of his carriage. They sat silently together as the carriage took them out to the north-east.

Kleve watched with some distaste as the lights grew dimmer and the streets grew quieter and dingier.

Frankenstein saw his expression and sat silently watching.

Just outside the city gate he hauled his horse to a stand-still and the two men alighted. Frankenstein took Kleve's arm and guided him across the road into a rubble-filled yard and through a pair of rusty iron gates that had long since forgone their ability to open and close and now hung drunkenly on their hinges.

The men's steps echoed hollowly as they crossed the stone of the yard toward the shadow of the tumbledown building. Kleve looked at the building, and was about to ask how could they work in a place of such dilapidation, when Frankenstein indicated a set of steps leading downward between the outer wall and the wall of the building.

They walked down the uneven stone flags and Kleve realized that Frankenstein was beginning to walk a little faster with each step. They descended one flight, two flights, turned a corner, and arrived into a pool of light from a flickering lamp which was hidden completely from the street and the yard above. A few more steps down and they were faced by a door. Peeling paint formed its surface and the metal on it was rusted, but it was still solid.

Frankenstein reached for the bell-pull at the side of the door; soon the sound of shuffling steps could be heard coming to the door.

"Possibly not an ideal setting for a laboratory," said Frankenstein as they waited for the door to open. "But finding it was a stroke of luck, it is ideal for my . . . I beg your pardon, *our* purposes.

With a clattering of keys in the lock the door was opened to them, revealing a heavy surly man whose breath told of to close a friendship with the brandy bottle.

"Evening, Doctor." He opened the door and stood aside. They entered and Kleve felt his heart give a little jump at the sight of the painted door at the end of the short passage. Through this door was the private world of Baron Frankenstein.

Set in the heavy-bound door was a grille covering a peep-hole. Frankenstein advanced and banged on the door. The trap flicked open and for a moment there was a glimpse of an eye peering out, then the door swung open.

The two men moved forward and into the laboratory which had been created in the one-time wine store.

Kleve was fascinated as he stepped inside and there was revealed to him a laboratory such as he never dreamed could have existed.

There were instruments which he recognized and there were others which he did not. From behind came a sudden crash; he jumped, and turned to realize that it was the heavy door which had been shut and it was with something of a shock that he saw, staring at him warily, the twisted figure of the hunchback.

Frankenstein, who was already peeling off his gloves and cape, saw Kleve and the hunchback staring at each other. He addressed the hunchback.

"Karl, this is Dr. Hans Kleve. He is to work with us."

The hunchback with his queer sidling walk moved to Frankenstein's side, keeping his eyes on Kleve all the while.

"Do we really need him?" His voice was soft and surprisingly well modulated, it hardly seemed to belong to the bent form from which it emerged. He spoke quietly; his words were only for Frankenstein.

"Yes. I shall need an assistant and Dr. Kleve has come at just the right moment."

The dwarf looked worried and undecided. Hans felt it was time for him to break the ice.

"The Doctor trusts me and I hope you will too, Karl."

For a moment longer the hunchback summed up Kleve and looked again at Frankenstein, who nodded. Karl was content to follow the lead of the man who to him was the greatest in the world. As best he could with his part-paralysed face, he smiled.

Frankenstein led the way into the laboratory. There were two large benches clearly used for surgery. There were rows of cages of rabbits and rats. In the far corner there was a cage containing a live monkey. In the other corner were the doors of a large furnace. Near to it were more ordinary work benches with electrical devices. The wires from these all led to the centre of the room, and then disappeared behind a screen that hung from ceiling to floor. Kleve looked round realizing that, although there appeared no conscious effort at order, the whole of the laboratory seemed to centre itself round the screen and what it concealed.

"Come along, I'll show you round. Now this is Otto, our chimp," said Frankenstein by the monkey's cage.

"Otto was one of my very first experiments. His brain is not his own; it originally belonged to another monkey."

Otto was jumping up and down on his perch and Karl, the hunchback, came over in answer to his chattering and threw him a banana. Otto peeled it and returned to his quiet munching.

Frankenstein continued: "He had a wife at one time, but unfortunately he killed her and, as you can see, he gets upset if he doesn't get what he wants fairly quickly."

The continued round the laboratory, Frankenstein commenting here and explaining there, until they came to a large bench almost covered with electrical apparatus. On it were three covered jars. Kleve's curiosity crept ahead of his manners.

"What have you under there?" he asked.

"Ah, now that, Kleve, is a brain. All that is the best of my own construction. Let me demonstrate it to you."

He lifted the cover off the first tank and revealed to Kleve's gaze, a hand—a woman's hand floating in the tank of liquid. It was severed at the wrist, and from the now bloodless stump there ran a network of flexible tubes and wires which were connected to the main electrical apparatus on the bench.

"If you burn your hand in a flame, what makes you snatch it away?" asked Frankenstein.

"The nerves, of course." Kleve was puzzled.

"Exactly," said Frankenstein. "The nerves. The nerves send a message to the brain and the brain activates the muscles, withdrawing the hand. But you don't put your hand too near the flame if you see it first."

Kleve nodded.

"The eyes recognize fire as a source of pain and danger."

Frankenstein was alight with enthusiasm for what he was explaining. He lifted the cover off a second tank, revealing floating in it a pair of eyeball, pale and bloodless and, like the stump of the hand, connected to the electrical brain on the bench.

"Now observe this."

Frankenstein went round the bench plugging in and switching on the circuit until the apparatus was crackling and humming. Then he went over and picked a taper out of a drawer and lit it, shading it from any draught with his hand. Still shading it with his hand, he placed it in front of the tank containing the eyes.

"Watch the eyes."

Saying this, he removed his screening hand from the flame of the taper and slowly moved the taper across the sight of the eyes.

Kleve watched fascinated as the eyeballs in the tank slowly swivelled, watching the flame as it passed. Unlike normal eyes, they had no lids and they stared at the flame which was passing nearer to the tank containing the severed hand.

Frankenstein brought the taper in front of the tank with the hand, The eyes kept their gaze fixed on the taper flame with a hideous singleness of purpose. Frankenstein pushed the taper closer to the tank containing the stump of hand and as he watched, the hair began to rise on Kleve's spine.

The hand began to move. At first idly pressing backwards; then as the flame approached closer, it thrashed about in a frenzy of effort to retreat from the danger which threatened it.

The taper was pushed almost to the edge of the tank and the hand was nearly out of the liquid in its twisting, writhing efforts to get away. Suddenly Frankenstein blew out to taper, and in a moment the hand was floating peacefully once more in its tank. There was nothing but the ripples of the disturbed liquid to show that it had ever been anything other than the dead, severed stump that it was.

"Fascinating, isn't it?" Frankenstein pinched the end of the taper and dropped it back into the bench drawer.

"This is a brain?" he asked.

Kleve's brow was moist and his mouth felt a little dry.

"Of a sort, yes." Frankenstein waved his hand at the mass of apparatus on the bench. "But with all this paraphernalia it is still capable of only one reaction." He turned to Kleve. "Can you imagine the complexity of the human brain? One tenth of the size and a million times more efficient. It controls every action, every reaction. It stores memories, it motivates all life. . . . And this is all I have been able to do."

Kleve had recovered from the initial shock at seeing these bits of flesh 'come to life'. "I have never seen anything like it."

"No, I don't suppose you have," said Frankenstein, "and nor have you seen anything like this. Come here."

He moved toward the tall screen which dominated the laboratory. When Frankenstein reached it he put his hand up to the screen and turned to face Kleve.

"You know that Frankenstein was condemned to death?"

Hans Kleve nodded.

"You know what for?"

Kleve nodded again. "The story has become a legend. Frankenstein constructed a man who became a monster . . .!"

"It should have been perfect," Frankenstein's voice cut in harsh with emotion. "I made it to be perfect. If the brain hadn't been damaged, my work would have been hailed as the greatest scientific achievement of all time. Frankenstein would have been accepted as a genius of science. Instead he was sent to the guillotine. I swore then that they would never be rid of me."

Tense with feeling he jerked back the screen.

"Now this is something I am proud of."

Kleve's eyes slowly widened.

In front of him was an enormous, tall glass tank, the contents of which all the time fumed and gently bubbled. His eyes followed the sides up to the top, which was some fourteen feet above the floor.

Suspended in the liquid, and gently swaying to and fro in the eddies that formed, was the body of a tall, well-built man. Kleve slowly lowered his gaze.

The lower part of the body was swathed in bandages but the magnificent torso was clear in all its curing muscle. The top of the head was bandaged. The eyes and the face were peculiarly without expression.

They were open, yet curiously unseeing. Kleve was awed.

This was beyond his wildest dreams. "Who is he?" he whispered.

"Nobody. He isn't born yet. He has no brain to bring life to him, but this time he is perfect. Except for a few scars here and there, he is perfect."

"He is not alive?"

"Not yet."

"You made this from other bodies?"

Frankenstein nodded and drew the screens back across the glass tank and its slowly-swaying contents.

"My voluntary work at the hospital serves me very well. All I need now is a brain, and then I can give it life. Until then he remains in what I call my 'keeping fluid'".

They moved slowly back among the benches where the electric brain with its hand and eyeballs was situated. Frankenstein pointed to the experimental brain on the bench.

"Look at the size of this. It is impossible for me to construct a brain. Unlike the limbs, it is impossible to restore life once life is gone. It must be a living brain. The brain is life, so a living brain must be found." Kleve was shocked in spite of the fascination of his search for science.

"But that would be murder."

Frankenstein was unperturbed. "Not necessarily," he said. "I have a volunteer . . . here in the laboratory."

Kleve realized that Frankenstein was looking at him and smiling.

"No, my dear Hans, not you. Your brain is too valuable where it is . . . there he is—my volunteer."

With a wave of his hand Frankenstein indicated Karl, the hunchback, standing by the monkey's cage, where he was feeding the monkey.

"You mean Karl?"

Frankenstein leaned against the bench.

"Yes, he and I made a bargain. If he saved me from the guillotine, I would make him a new body."

"But surely that twisted hand and the paralysis indicates an injury to the brain?"

"I have examined him thoroughly. The paralysis is due to a blood clot. It can be dispersed during the operation. Karl has a fine brain." At the sound of his name the hunchback moved towards them with his dragging foot and his sideways shuffle.

"Yes, Karl is quick, and he has absorbed a great deal of knowledge while he has been with me, haven't you, Karl?"

"Dr. Stein," Karl said in his curiously soft voice, "is welcome to my brain, so long as he rids me of this," and his one mobile hand made a gesture sweeping from his head to his feet.

Kleve looked at the dwarf with a renewed interest. The man had courage. Here was a man who was willing to risk his life . . . to have life.

"You must have great faith in Dr. Stein,"

"I have," said the dwarf simply, and turned and shuffled back to the cage where the monkey was beginning to chatter its shrill rage at being ignored.

"Are you sure it can be done?" asked Kleve.

Frankenstein looked at Kleve intently.

"The operation will be a complete success; I have practised it too often to fail . . . Come, it is late. We must return, so that in the morning we shall be fresh to serve out to those who think they are ill, potions which they think will cure the ills which they do not have. All this research you know, my dear Hans, has to be paid for." As he slipped on his cape Frankenstein nodded at the apparatus which cluttered the laboratory.

But there was only one thing in the mind of Hans Kleve at that time.

"When are you going to do it?"

Frankenstein pulled on his gloves and held open the door. He looked over to where the glass tank was hidden behind the screens.

"Soon, now," he said. "Very soon."

Jimmy Sangster

CHAPTER THREE

FRANKENSTEIN, in spite of his passion for his work, was forced to let the weeks slip past until he was sure of the capabilities of hans Kleve. To have no assistant meant merely that life was a little difficult; to have an incompetent one would be a disaster.

He sent Kleve to spend most of his time in the hospital where he would learn, and in the evenings the two would travel out to the wine-cellar laboratory, where Frankenstein would pour his knowledge out in a luxurious stream for the eager Kleve.

Much of Kleve's practice had been transferred to Frankenstein's town surgery and, consequently, it was nothing out of the ordinary for Frankenstein to find unknown names on his consulting list for the day.

That day he swivelled himself to and fro in his chair, waiting for the receptionist to usher in the next patient. Whoever it was, they were late. He drew the appointment pad towards him and his lean finger traced down the list. It was a Miss Conrad, apparently, for whom he was waiting. For a minute or two he was not averse to relaxing, and looking out of the window at the bright sunny morning.

From his chair he could see through the window the trees, full of rich life. There were birds busying in and out of their branches intent on living their hardest. Over the garden wall he could hear the clop of horses' hooves as the town carriages and the tradesmen's van went on their morning errands. It was a world that was up and doing. It was a world of action—and he was forced to wait.

He clasped his hands and tapped his fingers together. Was he really forced to wait any longer? Hans had turned out to be better than he had hoped. The man had sopped up knowledge like a sponge, and his work with a knife was far beyond the average. But he still lacked an understanding of people. Frankenstein sighed. The big picture was still beyond Kleve's grasp. Kleve was concerned too much with the mechanics of the job, but as a mechanic he was excellent.

Frankenstein looked at the active world outside his window. Tonight it could be done, and that world could eat its words.

He dragged himself back to his task. Where was this confounded patient? Irritably he pressed the button which called his receptionist. If the woman wasn't there he would take the next patient and she would have to wait to the end of his surgery. If she came at all. Had he been able to see into the future he might have tried to avoid seeing this patient at all.

He was about to jab at the bell push when there was the quiet routine knock of his receptionist and the door opened to admit a vivacious young woman.

In spite of her youth she was obviously accustomed to authority, for she swept across the carpet towards his desk with a fresh assurance far beyond her years.

"Miss Conrad," murmured the receptionist, bowing himself out.

"Good morning, Doctor."

Frankenstein looked from the time on his watch to the time in his diary, and then to the young woman who had seated herself in front of him.

"Miss Conrad . . .? You are a few minutes late. What is the trouble, Miss Conrad?"

Margaret Conrad laughed.

"I am not a patient, Dr. Stein. . . . I come to offer my services."

Frankenstein swivelled from side to side in the chair behind the desk.

"I am afraid I don't quite understand."

"This voluntary work at your Poor Hospital interests me. I am not a trained curse, but I am sure there are many jobs I could do there."

Frankenstein groaned inwardly. Not only did he have to fend off matchmakers but, heavens above, a do-gooder. He preferred the hypochondriacs. It was much easier to get rid of them. All you had to do was give them a bottle of physic and they were happy. He cleared his throat deprecatingly.

"My dear Miss Conrad, I don't think you appreciate the nature, and er, conditions of our work at the Poor Hospital. It is very good of you to make the suggestion, but it is quite impossible.

Margaret Conrad was young enough to believe in revolution and beautiful enough not to have suffered much opposition as yet to her beliefs and desires. She bristled.

"Dr. Stein, it is time women were no longer regarded as something purely ornamental. I am sure I could be very useful and my aunt, the Countess Barcynska, told me you have so very little free time that I am certain you need someone to help."

"You live with the Countess?"

"I am staying with her for a few weeks. My parents live in the capital.

Frankenstein rose to his feet, straining hard to be politeness itself.

"I am sure your aunt can find other good works for you to do." He started to move round the side of the desk. "Please give her my regards."

Margaret Conrad sat unmoving in her chair.

"I shall be at the hospital at nine o'clock in the morning, Doctor."

Frankenstein was irritated.

"Miss Conrad! I thought I made it quite clear that your services are not required."

The girl sat without making any effort to move, and primped the lace collar round her throat.

"I fear that you have an exaggerated opinion of your position in this matter, Doctor." She brushed some invisible dust from the velvet of her sleeve. "My father is the Minister responsible for all hospitals and asylums; it is his signature on the licence which permits them to operate. It is also his signature which can go on the letter which revokes the licence . . . My father has agreed that I shall work for you." She flicked a final invisible speck from her sleeve. "And my father is very fond of me, he grants my every wish," she smiled a dazzling smile up at him. "So you see you really have no choice, Doctor Stein."

She gathered her things together and stood up, putting her hand out to him.

"Nine o'clock, Doctor?"

Frankenstein considered his position. The local Medical Council he could afford to snap his fingers at, but a Minister of State was a force to be reckoned with. He could not risk a fuss, or the closing of his hospital. He needed it far too much. He inclined his head. "As you say, Miss Conrad, I have no choice." He bowed over her hand.

"Do not worry, Doctor, I shall not interfere with your work."

Coldness fell down over him like a cloak. "You will have no opportunity, I assure you. . . . Good morning, Miss Conrad."

For a moment Margaret paused, then closed her mouth. What point was there in arguing. She had achieved what she had set out to do, and there would be ample time to instruct Dr. Stein in his manners later.

Margaret Conrad picked up her skirts and swept out.

Once she was outside the porch and the doctor's door was closed behind her, she indulged in a couple of joyous skips of glee on her way down the steps to the carriage.

Her father was indeed the Minister of Health; but the possibility of his daughter working in a Poor Hospital would have given him apoplexy. She would have to be careful that Auntie Barcynska didn't accidentally let the cat out of the bag.

Boris, the footman, helped her up into her open carriage, and as he folded the steps she told him:

"Take me to the Poor Hospital, Boris."

The landau jogged through the streets and pulled up outside a building which, Margaret noticed could have done with the attention of the painters. She descended and swept her way into a dim-lit lobby where, for a minute, she stood looking about and waiting for someone to attend to her.

The skinny figure of Slensky, the general factotum, detached itself from behind a little porter's alcove. He approached her wonderingly, with a brush in his hand.

"I want to see Dr. Kleve," said Margaret.

Slensky gaped at her but made no move.

"This is the Poor Hospital, isn't it?"

The figure nodded, leaning on its brush.

"Dr. Kleve does work here?"

The figure nodded once more.

"Well, I want to see him."

The figure at last come to life. It straightened up and suddenly, as it scuttled away, proclaimed:

"Er, yes, Miss, I'll get him."

The up-patient pushed open the door to the ward and a babble of sound floated out into the lobby as he moved inside. He edged his way in between the beds to where Hans Kleve was putting a new dressing on a patient's side. The factotum took an interested glance at the hole in the flesh that Hans was dressing, and then confidentially he leaned toward the doctor.

"Someone asking for you, Dr. Kleve, . . . a real lady. . . she's got scent on."

Hans finished tying the bandage over the dressing.

"She must have come to the wrong surgery."

He climbed to his feet and wiped his hands. As he moved toward the door, Slensky called after him:

"I put ='er in the Doctor's room."

Kleve hurried toward the office. He could not afford to let patients run away and if she thought this was his normal office there would be little likelihood of her paying a second visit. He turned the handle of the door, ready to pour out his apologies.

By the cabinet there was a slim figure dressed in dark velvet. She turned and before he could utter a word she gave him a smile.

"Good morning. Are you Dr. Kleve?"

Hans recovered himself slightly.

"Er, yes, good morning."

"I am Margaret Conrad. I shall be working here."

Although Hans was becoming acutely aware of two things, the deep violet of the eyes that seemed to pull at him and the fact that he was in his dirtiest overall, he was still sufficiently cautious not to jump into anything that affected his work.

"Doctor Stein hasn't mentioned anything to me."

"My father is the Minister of Health . . . Dr. Stein has been informed."

"I see," said Hans, not seeing at all, except that he wished all his visitors took this particular shape.

"I shall read to the sick, shop for them, get them tobacco, writing paper, soap. . . ."

Hans Kleve stifled a smile somewhat ineffectively.

"My dear lady," he said, "they rarely wash, they cannot write and they have no money to buy tobacco."

She looked so hurt that immediately he had said it, he wished he had not, and he hastily added:

". . . I am sure you will find plenty to do."

"Thank you," said Margaret. "I won't disappoint you."

They stood staring at each other for a long moment until the door of the office suddenly opened and the twisted figure of Karl sidled quickly in. He was in a state of elation.

"Dr. Kleve, I was told. . . . Oh!"

He stopped short on seeing that Hans was not alone. His eyes remained fixed on Margaret.

"Karl, this lady is going to help us here."

Margaret favoured the hunchback with a smile which left him transfixed. Without thinking, she offered him her hand to shake, and then was forced to cover her embarrassment when he could only move his left hand out to acknowledge her.

Neither Hans nor Margaret knew it, but at that moment Karl was deep on his way into a dream world. A world where women smiled at him and he walked with a firm stride, women like this one with her velvet skin and her delicate perfume. Women he could pursue and who would want to be pursued by him after the miracle which was now so near, the miracle of his new body.

Hans broke into the daydream.

"Did you want something, Karl?"

"I wanted to tell you . . ." he broke off and smiled; he could afford to be happy.

". . . no, it does not matter."

"If it is a professional matter, I can leave you." said Margaret, smiling at him graciously.

He smiled in return at her, and because at this time he lived in a seventh heaven of expectation, in spite of its twisted awkwardness, his smile was almost shy and charming.

"No. . . . Please do not disturb yourself, Dr. Kleve will understand if I just say that Dr. Stein wants you to be sure that you are free *to-night—to-night*," he repeated and as he backed out of the room his eyes shone.

As the door closed behind him Margaret clapped her hands to her face and turned to Hans.

"I feel dreadful. When I offered him my hand I didn't realize."

"He seemed quite taken with you," said Hans.

"Is he a patient?"

Hans paused for a moment before answering.

"Er . . . he helps Doctor Stein." He caught her look of surprise. "There is a very sound brain in that unfortunate body, and perhaps soon we might even be help him in that respect."

This was getting near to dangerous ground, and he pulled himself back.

"Are you *quite* sure you want to work here?"

"Quite sure . . . it is far to late to try to put me off now. I told Dr. Stein I should be here in the morning."

He escorted her out of the office down to her carriage and watched her drive away into the sunshine. Self-possessed, assured, and, he hated to have to admit it, perhaps a tiny bit stupid.

But through the day one thing burned in his mind. It was the one word that Karl the hunchback had repeated with such a light in his eyes: "To-night".

Karl could only have meant one thing.

To-night they would start work on the most important experiment of all. The transfer of Karl to his new body.

Hans could not wait for his day of routine at the hospital to end. The round of stitching gashes, packing stubs and listening at the chests seemed unending. Finally he was able to throw off his overall and, grabbing his coat, slipping his arms into it as he ran, he tore down to the street.

The cab could not go fast enough for him. He almost ran into Frankenstein's surgery. The receptionist was putting on his coat and in the consulting room, Frankenstein was already in his street clothes and checking a small case of instruments.

"Ah, there you are, my dear Hans. I thought you were never coming. Did you have that dreadful young woman come down to see you at the hospital today?"

"Yes. Karl said . . ."

"You know, she wants to do some work or other. I did my best to dissuade her, but her father is the Minister of Health. It would be very inconvenient if anything were to jeopardize the hospital."

"She seems a very determined young lady. Tell me, when Karl came in. . ."

"Get her to wash one of the patients. That should deter her sufficiently. Are you ready?"

"Stein, stop evading the point. Where are we going and I want to know for certain, what are we doing tonight?"

Frankenstein's grey eyes glittered; he was in high humour. He snapped the instrument case shut.

"We go to the laboratory. Tonight we give Karl his new body."

The two men climbed into Frankenstein's brougham and set off toward the centre of town. However, instead of going to the laboratory, Frankenstein turned off in the direction of the Poor Hospital.

"Why have you turned off?" asked Hans.

"We go to the hospital to collect the ambulance. We can't leave

Karl in the laboratory after tonight. We shall have to have him right under our noses where we can look after him."

The brougham rolled neatly into the hospital yard and Frankenstein took it round by the out-house. They descended and Frankenstein called for the ostler.

"Hey there, Mark!"

The man came out from the kitchens wiping his mouth.

"Dr. Stein, What are you doing here this time of an evening?"

"Mark. I want you to harness up the ambulance for me. Dr. Kleve and I will drive it; there is a patient we may have to collect."

Mark brought out the worldly-wise old cob that was used for hauling the ambulance, and backed it into the shafts. The cob tapped his heels on the paving stones, slightly irritated at being dragged out of his routine, but still sufficiently phlegmatic to accept it all as part and parcel of life.

The doctors transferred the instruments cases into the ambulance and climbed up onto the box waiting for Mark to fasten the last buckle. Finally the old ostler gave the horse a slap on the flank, rubbed him loosely by the ears and said, as much to the horse as to the two men sitting on the box:

"You're all ready to go now. . . ."

He called after the old vehicle as it rumbled out of the yard: "Good-night".

When the two men reached the laboratory they found the curtains drawn and Karl standing by the big tank watching his new body swinging slightly in the slings the suspended it.

He was so absorbed that he didn't hear them come in. He was walking slowly round the tank peering up at his new image as though he were trying to familiarize himself with it.

Here and there on the body were the faint marks of scars where the segments had joined together. They were no more than streaks and if the limbs were marked it mattered nothing to Karl; at least they were straight.

Frankenstein and Kleve had almost reached the end of the bench when Karl heard them and turned round.

Frankenstein placed his case of instruments on the bench.

"All ready, Karl?"

"I'm ready, Doctor," said Karl, coming forward and taking

Frankenstein's cloak from him. He hung it up by the cupboard. Frankenstein turned to Hans.
"You know where most of the things are, so I leave you to get your side of the things ready."

Frankenstein pulled over a small trolley to the side of the operating table and began to set out a tray of instruments. Methodically he laid them out in the groups which he knew they would have to be used. There were clips, knives, and scalpels of a shape which were then unknown elsewhere. All to cover a technique and a knowledge beyond the scope of the rock-coated butchers, whose work Frankenstein regarded as being so backward as to be amateur.

The instruments lay glistening wickedly, the very angles of their blades proclaiming their sharpness. They winked in the light as the table shook slightly.

The dwarf had returned and was watching as Frankenstein's hands swiftly laid the trays of instruments in their patterns. His eyes were morbidly drawn to the knives which would sever his body.

Frankenstein sensed the imaginings that were flitting through Karl's mind, and took him by the shoulder. He steered him to the tank where the new body was suspended.

"Keep looking at him, Karl . . . in a few hours, that will be you."

The laboratory was soon ready. The two operating tables had been placed close to each other, with the shining array of knives and needles on the trolley between them. Clean white sheets covered the two tables, and at the foot of each was neatly folded a thick, warm blanket.

The only difference between these twin tables was that waiting at the head of one of them stood a frame of cables and wires connected at one end to a great power pack, and at the other a single, metal electroded head-piece.

Frankenstein moved to where the dwarf was still standing looking at his image in the tank.

"We are ready for him now. Do you want to help us make him ready?"

The dwarf tore his eyes from the tall, straight figure and choked.

"Yes. . . . I want to help. All the time till it is done, I want to help.

Together the three of them raised the figure out of its tank, and the smell of the fluid fumes seeped stronger through the laboratory. The brought the body down and laid it in place on its table. I was cold, ice cold, but they wrapped it warmly for the time when life should course through the veins.

Karl was no longer afraid, his hands were trembling, his eyes were shining, he was exalted.

Frankenstein sent him to undress and then he told Hans: "Go up and tell Kloster to go off for the night. I want no one here who doesn't need to be here. Stay and watch until he leaves. Give him a couple of gold pieces if you want. Tonight he can go and get as drunk as he likes; anything. so long as he is away out of sight and out of earshot."

Kleve did as he was told and tipped a couple of coins into the man's hand. Kloster was nothing loath to leave his post to sup his brandy in a tavern. Besides, he knew that tonight was an important night, and sometimes the sounds that came from the laboratory, through the closed door, were such as he would prefer to be absent when the doctor had one of his important experiments on hand.

Kleve watched the lumbering figure clamber up the stairs and waited until he could hear the steel-tipped boots crossing the courtyard far above before he locked and barred the doors. First the outer door, and then the thick, studded door which lead to the laboratory itself.

By the time he returned, the dwarf was already lying in his appointed place and Frankenstein was in his whitest of overalls.

"Get into your things, Hans," said Frankenstein. "We are waiting."

Hans washed up, put on his overalls, and moved to the head of the table where the dwarf lay.

Frankenstein nodded to him, and then addressed the dwarf.

"Now you must be calm, Karl. You will sleep and while you sleep, we will rid you of this," he touched the dwarf's hunch. "Remember, breathe deeply and sleep, Karl.

Kleve carefully dripped the anæsthetising fluid into the mask of padding and lowered it onto the dwarf's face. He had never found out the constituents of the doctor's anæsthetic, but it was more sure than anything he had ever been shown in medical school.

Frankenstein watched as the dwarf's breathing deepened into unconsciousness.

"I rely on you," he said to Hans. "He must go as far down as it is possible for him to go, but you must not push him over the edge. His system must be numb to its core, but his brain must still be living when it leaves his body." They stood waiting while the dwarf's breathing grew deeper and slower.

"He's ready now," said Kleve.

Frankenstein bent, checking the reactions and the pulse. He nodded.

"Help me turn him on his side."

The two of them twisted the shoulders over, then with lightning speed, Frankenstein began his work.

At first he worked with speed alone, caring little of what was left behind, then as he went deeper he began to slow and work with more care.

With infinite delicacy he drilled the holes in the bones through which he could insert the saws to do their job, rubbing away the tissue with a sound like running a finger nail along the side of a brick. A soft muted sound of a hard edge rubbing on a soft edge, a pulpy sound.

The organ was exposed, and Frankenstein cursed; there was little room for him to work.

"Why don't you make a bigger cut?" asked Hans.

"I want his face whole, so that the body can be recognized as his. I had wanted to be neat, but this way we shall have to be very quick; the shock may kill him."

Frankenstein's face contorted with effort. There was a sound of snapping bone and the form under the sheet gave a babbling moan. Its breath came in long, unsteady gasps.

Frankenstein worked at a frenzy until, with an almost loving touch, he was able to lift out the pulpy mass he was seeking. Gently he place it onto a kidney dish, then with the most difficult part of his work past, he felt faint from the reaction.

"Hans," he gasped, "you have the 'keeping fluid'—put it in—my hands are too unsteady at this moment."

The glass jar of fluid was ready, waiting. Gently, so gently, Hans tilted it until the living tissue slid into the fluid. The severed brain of the hunchback slowly settled to the bottom of the jar, tinting the water with the pink trace of blood.

When Hans had done this he turned and watched as Frankenstein made injections into the barely alive form.

"Embalming fluid, my dear Hans. Karl's body must be kept for posterity to see.

Although his face was still running with sweat, Frankenstein seemed to have once more an iron hold on himself.

"We will have a little rest, and then we can complete this work. But first we cure Karl's limp."

With the brain still submerged in fluid he worked and dissipated the cause of the paralysis.

It was hours of patient labour of placing, before the brain was in its new abode, and the top of the skull fastened in its place to the satisfaction of the fastidious Frankenstein.

The tall form on the operating table lay still as marble. The brain was in there, the brain which was living, but the body still looked as cold and dead as when it had been hanging in its tank.

Hans wheeled the trolleys away and watched Frankenstein connect the wires of the energizer, wondering at the cold mask of the face of the body. Could they have been wrong? Could Frankenstein have been wrong? Could he, Dr. Hans Kleve of Karlsbruck, have connived and abetted= a murder. To tear the brain out of a man and place it in a corpse that never lived! If they failed, people would call it the work of madmen.

Now that the cutting and the binding had been done Frankenstein seemed supremely confident.

"Hurry, Hans. I want you to keep an eye on him while I start things up. We have to bring these cells to life, to energize them. What the world outside calls the miracle of life is no longer a miracle, but a simple scientific formula."

The frame was wheeled into position and the metal headband clamped round the new body of Karl. While Hans felt for the non-existent pulse, Frankenstein started the energiser and it crackled its current through the circuits.

Frankenstein, as he pushed the last switch into place, clicked a stop-watch into motion and picked up the other wrist.

The noise and crackle of the sparks meant that they had to rely on their senses of touch to recognise that first feeble spurt of life as the blood was pushed round the body.

The seconds grew into a minute but Frankenstein seemed unperturbed, and then, simultaneously, both men stiffened. Kleve tried not to grip too hard in his excitement . . .it came, just once . . . and then a long pause . . . one pulse-beat, then again, again and quicker.

There was life in the new Karl.

The two men grinned happily at each other. The pulse was slow but it was steady. Frankenstein adjusted the energiser.

"It's all over now," he said. "You might as well go on with the cleaning up."

Hans busied himself with the trays and the instruments. Then as he was turning over the far side of the table he first saw it move.

It was only a flicker of a finger but it caught his eye. The hand on the opposite side to where Frankenstein was standing began to move jerkily upwards.

"Look! The hand!"

He began to run but he was too late.

The hand waved up toward the head and caught straight into the maze of wires, the body writhed, and a frightful scream rent the air.

"Aaaaaaaaah! Asssssssh!"

"Quick! The anæsthetic!" shouted Frankenstein.

Frankenstein pulled at the hand on the wire and was thrown to the ground.

The current flashed and the screams rent the air. Frankenstein crashed the main switch over, and by then Hans had reached the head of the table with his mask of volatile anæsthetic. Under the mask, the moans died down until the body was quiet save for occasional twitches.

"Thank God the pulse is still there. We must strap him down!"

"Poor Karl," said Frankenstein, "he must have been in agony." Frankenstein leaned back and surveyed the deep struggling breathing of the body.

"How long before the brain will have any control?"

"A few hours yet. The brain is completely anæsthetised again. When he regains consciousness the brain will take some time to adjust itself to his new body. He must have complete rest and avoid any sudden movements. As a precaution I shall keep him strapped for a time, even after he is awake."

Hans stared at the now quietly breathing figure.

"I would never have believed it possible."

Frankenstein smiled and patted Hans on the arm.

"Thank you for your assistance, Hans. This is only the beginning of our work together."

"There was a chattering sound behind them. Frankenstein laughed.

"Ha, it's Otto! He must want his dinner, and now there is no Karl to give it to him. We shall have to share some extra work, you and I, until Karl is on his feet."

The feeding of Otto completed, Frankenstein returned to the problem of Karl.

"I want to get him back to the hospital. Go upstairs, Hans, and bring the stretcher down from the ambulance."

Hans was happy to put his head out into the night. The air was clean and cool and the atmosphere of the laboratory was hot and stifling with the smell of the life fluid. For a while he paused, drinking in the fresh air.

With considerable difficulty the two of them worked their way up the flights of stairs to the courtyard with the stretcher in between them, tilted steeply but always held gently and smoothly against any possibility of a jar.

As they loaded the form into the back of the tall, old-fashioned, horse ambulance, which was the best the Poor Hospital could boast, the horse gave a sudden jerk and the stretcher slip a little in their hands.

"Is he all right?" asked Hans.

"Yes," Frankenstein said, "but go carefully."

They jogged through the silent, dark streets. Hans was at the reins and Frankenstein inside the ambulance, holding the head in its cocoon of bandages to prevent it from rolling too much in the bumping over the cobbles.

At the Poor Hospital, they managed to get the stretcher in the main door and up the stairs past Stein's office without rousing any of the staff.

They put the stretcher down outside the attic door, and Frankenstein fumbled in his pocket for the keys. Even as he pressed the key into the lock there came from the stretcher a wild animal cry that echoed round the dusty corridor.

In his side room Slensky shot up in his bed. He heard voices and a moaning, and it wasn't coming from the ward.

He slipped out of his bed and crept up the stairs but there was nothing on the first landing. He crept up the stairs but there was nothing on the first landing. He crept up the next flight in his stockinged feet, and as he reached the top, a shuddering moan froze him in his steps.

He crept up the last steps and carefully peered round the balustrade at the top of the stairs.

There was Dr. Stein and Dr. Kleve, and between them they were lifting a stretcher and taking it into the room. From the stretcher came moans, and the keen, ferret-eyes of Slensky noted that the figure in the stretcher was held down by straps.

The two doctors struggled in with the weight of the body and lifted it into the bed. "Get the straps off the stretcher," said Frankenstein. "We can use those."

They put the straps round Karl's body and again one to each wrist.

As they laid him in the bed Karl was moaning.

"Gently, Karl, relax. You are quite safe."

"Sleep now, Karl, you must sleep."

He turned to Hans. "Poor chap, he is bound to have pain as the anæsthetic wears off, but he must not move or damage that brain of his.

"There is nothing more we can do now until the morning. We will go down to the office."

Hans began to realise how tired he was. The two doctors quietly walked out of the attic, locked the door behind them, and quietly descended the far staircase, unaware that they were doing all this under the eager, watchful curious gaze of Slensky.

CHAPTER FOUR

FOR a week, Frankenstein and Hans were tied to the hospital. One of them was always within reach of the room where Karl's brain was gradually taking control in his new body.

The attic room was kept locked, and they performed all the services of nursing.

As this week passed, Slensky who, with his mobility, prided himself on his knowledge of everything that went on, became consumed with the curiosity to see who was so closely guarded, and what it was that caused those screams which were muffled behind the door in the attic, and which caused either one of the two doctors to go rushing up from the office.

Time and again as he brought in the doctor's tray of lunch or swept out the office, Slensky almost too the chance of seeking the key; to open the door and peep inside the attic.

But each time his courage failed him, and his ferret brain excused itself by saying that if, when he opened the door, the patient screamed, then the key would be found to be missing and the fat would be in the fire. He had no illusions that the matter would not quickly be traced to him. But for him to be in ignorance of what went on in any part of the hospital was a burr pricking at his pride, and whenever one of the two doctors was due to take in a meal or make a routine call he hung around in the hope that sometime one would leave the door ajar.

That morning, he carried in the jug of water to the office and the little tray of food, and stood there waiting for Dr. Stein with the tray in his hand.

"Thank you, Slensky, leave it on the desk, will you?" said Frankenstein.

"Oh, it's all right, Doctor, I don't mind waiting; I'll carry it up for you."

Frankenstein raised his eyes and fastened them coldly on Slensky.

"Put it on the desk."

Slensky squirmed under the gaze and hastily lowered the items on to the desk. He stepped back, rubbing his grubby hands on his pants.

"No offence, Doctor Stein, I just like to help as much as I can."

The glance at him was coldly unsympathetic, so Slensky clutched a hand under his heart, coughed and added: "That is, while I can," and backed out of the room.

Frankenstein walked along the corridor and poked his head into the ward. He called to Hans Kleve and jerked his head to indicate that he was going up to the attic.

"Hans," he called, "would you bring up the dressing tray?"

Kleve abandoned the charts he was reading and went out of the ward through the door which Frankenstein was holding open.

Each carrying a tray, they trudged up to the attic room. Frankenstein talked over his shoulder as they ascended the creaking stairs.

"Today, I think we shall be able to leave off the dressing round his head. The wound should be healed. Also I want to try to instil into his mind the idea that he is not to be an invalid, but that soon he must get up and walk."

They paused outside the door and, balancing the tray on one hand, Frankenstein kicked the door open as the catch grated free.

As they entered the room, Frankenstein slipped the key out of the lock and closed the door.

In the passage, the figure of Slensky disengaged itself from the shadow and tip-toed to the door of the attic room. He knelt down and applied his eye to the keyhole. He could see the corner of a bed and then from the inside of the room key was inserted in the lock and turned, cutting off his vision. It was useless for him to wait, so he retired down the stairs to his room, thoughtfully sucking his teeth.

When Frankenstein had locked the door from the inside, he and Hans crossed over to the bed and looked down at the sleeping figure.

Sensing their presence, the figure stirred, and its eyes flickered open. As the consciousness crept into them there came fear, and the body made violent jerks against the straps, as if trying to escape from control.

Frankenstein leaned over the figure on the bed so that he was clearly visible.

"It's all right, it is only me. Dr. Kleve is with me and we have brought you some food . . ."He leaned further over him. " Karl can you hear me?"

At last the figure relaxed, although it was still trembling and the eyes turned to Frankenstein. It was a baby there is nothing unusual about its inability to form words, for the brain is not co-ordinated with the body. Karl was in a similar condition. He knew what he wanted to say but he could not yet force his body to produce the words.

The mouth opened, closed and opened, and all that emerged was a strangled gurgle. Frankenstein patted him.

"Don't worry Karl, it will come. I am going to take off your head bandage."

Tears of effort ran down the face of the figure on the bed and he managed to make a controlled nod= of assent.

"Lift the head for me while I unwind the bandage," said Frankenstein, and he began gently to unwind the dressing that ran round the head of the man in the bed. He removed the bandage and came to the final pad that the bandage held in place.

Carefully, a fraction at a time, he pulled it gently away and with each inch his expression became less tense.

"Good, good." He looked into the eyes of the figure in the bed. "You have made wonderful progress in the last week. Today I have something for you which I hope will give you and idea of what you will be."

The bandages were entirely free and the two doctors leaned close to examine the head.

It was a lean, well proportioned head, and now the life was flickering in the eyes, it might even become an attractive head. It suffered only one defect. Running all the way across the forehead and disappearing into the hair at either side, was a thick, puckered scar. It was this that Frankenstein delicately explored with his fingers.

The figure twitched as he ran his hands round the skull.

"Hurt?" He looked down.

With an enormous effort the figure rolled its head from side to side. Then it tugged a little at the straps, seeing the doctor's attention was still on it.

Frankenstein understood. "These are still necessary for a while, Karl . . . I'm sorry, but it will not be for long. We dare not risk a sudden movement which might break some newly healed piece of you. I will give you your food now."

He went to collect the tray and beckoned Hans over to him.

"Hans, I want to give him something which will stimulate his will to live. Downstairs in the office there is a cardboard box on the top of the chemical cupboard. I want you to bring it up here."

Hans took the key from Frankenstein's hand, unlocked the door and slipped downstairs to the office. The box was large, and looked oddly out of place amid the litter of bottles that stood in the chemical corner. He picked it up and started out the door. He was just closing it behind him when he became aware of a figure gliding quickly toward him.

Margaret Conrad came up to him and with an exaggerated curtsey bid him, "Good morning, Dr. Kleve."

For a moment Hans didn't know whether to carry on his course upstairs or to pause, but he was a young man, and when Miss Conrad took time to smile and curtsey, it was very unusual for any young man to go unthinking on his way.

"Er, good morning," he said. "So you are still with us, Miss Conrad?"

"Of course, did you think I would be frightened away by now?"

"I—er, no, but Dr. Stein did."

"I am interested in the patients."

"It's very unusual—I mean in a place like this."

"I could ask you why you work in a place like this!" said Margaret Conrad.

"I admire Doctor Stein, he is a fine man." As if the mention of the name brought his errand back to his mind he started to edge past her toward the stairs.

"Well, we shall be seeing quite a lot of each other."

"We shall."

"Then I can set my mind at rest about your leaving?"

"Certainly," said Margaret.

"I'm so glad," he waved the parcel at her. "I must get on now; you must excuse me," and he bolted up the stairs to the attic.

Frankenstein was feeding the last of the morsels to Karl in the bed. He looked up over his shoulder as Hans entered the room.

"What kept you, couldn't you find it?"

"No, here it is. Incidentally, what is it?"

Frankenstein chuckled and looked infernally pleased with himself. He propped the head of the figure so it could see easily round the room.

"This is for you," he said, looking closely at Karl, with his eyes twinkling merrily. He took off the lid of the box, slid his hand in, and raised up the contents. He called to the figure in the bed.

"Look, Karl, your first new suit!"

He slipped the hanger through the coat and twisted it this way and that.

"You remember what I promised you, Karl? See, the back is cut flat and straight and it will fit!"

He came over and leaned on the foot of the bed. "You couldn't even get into your old clothes now. You used to be a little man. Karl, when you stand up from that bed you will be about the same height as Dr. Kleve here. Tall, but not too tall. Now, I am going to hang this suit up here and I want you to keep your eyes on it, and know that when you get on your feet you will be able to wear it."

They left the figure of Karl propped up in bed with his eyes glued to the modest suit of plain cloth that draped from its hanger on the wall. As they walked down the stairs, Kleve asked:

"Are you sure those clothes will fit him?"

"Of course I am sure, they are made to measure. I had them made nearly six months ago."

"But how did you know what size to order?"

Frankenstein looked at him and burst out laughing.

"My dear hans, aren't you forgetting. I don't see that the measurement for the suit should be any problem when you consider that, after all, I chose the measurements for the body that goes inside it."

Exactly as Frankenstein had hoped, the clothes hanging on their peg acted an incentive for Karl to put his every effort to progress.

Day by day he managed to get the muscles of his body better under control; and there were fewer of the sudden starts and shakes that used to rack his frame. But still he had to be his guard against them when he awoke.

There would be terrible moments when he was unable to relate anything that he could see to life itself, or even to understand that he was alive. At these times his body would twitch and writhe, until his brain once more gained its full consciousness and control.

Each morning, Frankenstein would accompany Hans, and they would test the reflexes before they went on to do the routine rounds of the wards.

That morning, Hans was holding the mirror while, with the light reflected from it, Frankenstein checked the reactions of the pupils in Karl's eyes.

Keep it steady on the right—now the left. . . . The reactions are good." Frankenstein undid the strap round the wrists.

"Now Karl, lift up your left hand."

After a momentary effort, Karl raised the arm and flexed it to and fro.

"Now the right one, Karl."

Frankenstein's face became tense as he watched this arm, the arm which in Karl's old body had been paralysed.

There was a fractionally longer pause and then the arm moved up steadily and under control, though it seemed be just a little sluggish in comparison with the action of the other arm. The slightest semblance of a frown flickered across Frankenstein's face, but nevertheless, when he said up straight on the edge of the bed, he said:

"Hmmm. There is really very little wrong with you Karl!"
He jerked his head at the clothes on the wall. "You will be wearing these before so very long!"

He stood up. "I had better go and do my rounds in the ward now. I shall be back soon, Karl. Dr. Kleve will see to you."

He beckoned Hans to the door and in an undertone he said: "Except for the movement of his right hand his reactions are excellent. Better than I had hoped. Don't over-tax him but try to keep his mind active while you are with him. Talk to him, then when he shows signs of fatigue give him one of these tablets. I shall go to the laboratory when I have finished on the ward. Send for me if you need me."

He patted the lock. "Don't forget to keep this locked."

For some time this insistence of Frankenstein in having the door locked had bothered Karl. Why should they worry so much about keeping him apart? Of course, he knew that he would never have been put in the ward, but sometimes he felt too much as though he were not so much the special patient as a special prisoner.

It would have been easier for him to get this clear in his own mind if he had not be so confused as to his body.

It had not been as he had expected. At first the body did not seem to belong to him at all. He could do nothing to control it; he was as much a prisoner inside his new body as the body was a prisoner in the attic.

He had dreamed of fine dreams where he would wake up tall and strong. He would walk and run and dance. Dance with women, talk with women who would no longer turn from his in loathing. He, too, would be able to make those little rendezvous where two would slip away from a dance-floor and return later flushed and smiling, and other people would look at them only because they were flushed and smiling.

They would be just two people in a crowd, all dancing.

Dreams of a lifetime. To be one man in a crowd. Then Karl's grasp of reality took a hold. Even though this body was doing his bidding, suppose it never developed the small skills that he had possessed before? New bodies required food and clothes and a place to sleep. During the time he had been waiting for his body to be made he had not minded working in Frankenstein's laboratory, but it was not a place where he wished to stay for ever.

For the doctor, the sight of flesh being carved was of no consequence, or the permanent smell of formalin, and that sickly effervescence coming from the tank. All these were but a means to an end; he had endured them and now he had achieved that end . . . his new body.

Then, for a dreadful moment he wondered: do they keep the door locked because the body is too horrible for anyone who is not a doctor to see? Had his operation been a failure, after all the pain he endured? God, the pain! It was still an effort for him to speak clearly and he slowly forced the words out.

"Dr. Kleve."

Hans Kleve was still writing his notes and comparing the chart.

"Yes Karl?"

The effort Karl was forced to use in speaking gave him additional time to control some of his emotions and slowly he enunciated. He must not give them any idea that he suspected there might be something wrong.

"When can I see my new body?"

"Very soon, now. I think you will be proud of it."

In a measure this answer set his mind at rest. Kleve was young, he was wild with enthusiasm for the work which Frankenstein had done, and he was too ingenuous by nature to be an accomplished liar. But because of this, his answer to Karl's next question sent a chill of impotent fury along Karl's spine.

"Dr. Kleve," Karl asked, "what is going to happen when after . . =?"

Unconscious of the powers he was to unleash, Hans Kleve made his notes and talked.

"Oh, there are great plans for you, Karl. Doctors and scientists will come from all over the world to see you and talk to you.

Karl made a desperate attempt to explain.

"But, Doctor, all my life I have been a curiosity."

"It will be different now; you are in an important person. Dr. Stein intends to hold student lectures. They will see a normal man with a normal body compared side by side with your old body . . . You will play a great part in the advancement of science."

The words seared themselves into Karl's brain like letters burned with a red-hot poker. To be one of a crowd. To dance, to be like other people. All that he had gone through to be told that he was to be a peep-show for doctors. The muscles in his back and arms knotted as he writhed in bed.

Kleve dropped his notes and stood leaning over the form in the bed, his brow furrowed.

"Karl, are you in pain?"

Such pain as you will never understand, and not of the sort you can dull. Karl gradually managed to relax himself. The clouds of red cleared from in front of his vision and it was almost like his old, soft voice when he managed to gasp:

"No, no pain, Dr. Kleve."

Kleve fumbled in his pocket for the little box of pills that Frankenstein had given him. He shook one out into the palm of his hand, and poured a glass of water.

"Here, Karl, take this. You had better rest a little. You must not have too much excitement.

Karl swallowed the pill and leaned back. What matter if he swallowed another pill for them, he needed time to rest and time to think, but at least he knew now what he had to think about.

As Kleve left, he turned his head to the window and watched the clouds and occasional birds that flittered past to their nest under the eaves or away to the freedom of the fields.

Hans Kleve made his way down to the office and tidied up his papers; he also wanted a little time to think. There was a discreet cough.

" 'Ow's the special patient, doctor?" It was Slensky leaning on his broom.

Yes, how was the special patient? Kleve could no longer blind himself to the fact that there were things about Karl that worried him.

"What do you know about him?" Kleve asked sharply.

"Nothing, except that he is special. Is he all right? I mean, he makes a bit of noise, sometimes, don't he? Sounds like he gets regular upset."

Yes, that was what worried Hans. It was these terrible paroxysms that seemed to take hold of Karl without any real reason. If anything went slightly outside his control unreasoning fear would grip the body and it would fling itself about almost like the hand in the tank with its single reaction.

"He has been very ill, but he is getting along fine now," he lied comfortably. "When he is a little stronger we will probably shift him down into the ward with the other patients"

He had to talk to Frankenstein about this.

"Where is Dr. Stein?"

"He is in the ward, Doctor."

Kleve stood up from behind the desk and threw the bunch of keys into the drawer. He pushed the drawer shut and stalked out of the room to the ward.

Slensky watched him go and then noted, with a wolfish satisfaction, that the keys to the attic were kept in the second drawer from the top of the desk.

CHAPTER FIVE

FRANKENSTEIN was none too pleased at Hans Kleve's worries about the captive Karl. None to pleased, because if the truth were known, he too had similar misgivings; but he was sure, he told himself, that things would right themselves as the brain healed in its place.

After all, these furies were decreasing all the time. He had expected them, which was why he had used the straps to fasten Karl into his bed. He was irritated with Kleve as the young man forced the discussion on him in undertones while they did their work in the ward.

"We can't talk about this properly here, Hans. If it worries you so much, we will go down to the laboratory early tonight. Besides, there is something down there that I particularly want you to see."

Frankenstein stopped opposite an old man with a particularly rancid clay pipe stuck into his mouth.

"You're new here, aren't you?"

The old man nodded.

"What's your trouble?"

The old man took his pipe out of his mouth and tapped his chest with it.

"Me tubes," he said and placidly shoved the pipe back into his mouth.

"I'm not surprised," said Frankenstein, "since you appear to use yourself as an incinerator." He took the old man's pipe out of his mouth and dropped it into the waste-bin.

That's the first part of your cure," he said and moved on. Talking quietly to Hans as they moved from bed to bed, he suddenly said:

"While you have been spending time with Karl, I have been doing some work down at the laboratory. I told you Karl was only a beginning."

Then Frankenstein cut off his words. Coming into the ward gaily and suitably dressed in a pseudo-nurse's uniform was Margaret Conrad. Hooked on her arm was a basket of sundries. He couldn't stop her coming to the hospital, but at least he could prevent her from playing Lady

Bountiful while he was at work. If he had known the results of what he was going to say he would have gladly suffered her presence for the whole of the day, the whole of the week, the month if necessary, but instead he barked out:

"Miss Conrad!"

"Yes, Doctor?"

"I must ask you to confine your visits to such times as I am not actually at work in the ward."

He looked pointedly at the door. Margaret Conrad sensed that this was neither the time nor the place for a trial of strength. She inclined her head, albeit as gracefully as always and retired from the ward. Frankenstein caught sight of Slensky leaning on his broom, watching from the end of the ward, and more from the fact that he knew he had been caught out fighting with a girl, than because Slensky was constitutionally lazy, he snapped again:

"Haven't you anything to do?"

"Yessir!"

"Well do it, then."

"Yessir," repeated Slensky, and having more or less had his mind made up for him, he quickly nipped out of the ward into the corridor in the direction which Margaret Conrad had taken. He caught up with her in a few steps.

"Moody cove, ain't he?"

"I beg your pardon?"

Skensky clarified himself.

"Begging your pardon, Miss, I was meaning Dr. Stein—but then, if you knew what I knew!"

He stole a sideways glance at the girl.

"Cruel, he is."

The girl was frowning and deliberately not looking toward him, but Slensky knew he had around her interest.

"Cuts'em up he does. Alive!"

Margaret Conrad gave a little snort of disbelief.

"Don't talk such nonsense," she said.

"Let me tell you, Miss, they brought a new one in the other night. Terrible state he was in, all strapped down and screaming his head off."

"I don't believe a word you are saying," said Margaret Conrad, but her look belied her words. Slensky warmed to his task.

"You can see for yourself. He is kept in a special room up in the attic, all locked up."

Margaret Conrad looked at Slensky. He was a foxy-faced man, and a liar if ever she met one, but there was something about Dr. Stein, apart from his rudeness, which made her fell a little cold. She decided to settle it by calling Slensky's bluff.

"Just in case you're telling the truth, I think I had better see this man. You had better show me the way."

"'Course I will." He leered at her. Even if they found out now, he had the perfect excuse. After all, who was he to stop a lady, a real lady going where she wanted in the hospital.

"I know where they keep the key," he said. "They don't know I know, but then I know a lot of things that would surprise them.

He beckoned her down the corridor.

"You come with me. I'll get you the key.

Loath as she was to believe anything that this boxy creature could say, she had committed herself. By now she was determined that if there was a weapon she could use against Dr. Stein, then she wanted to be in a position to use it.

She gathered her skirts, and with a brief glance over her shoulder to be sure that the two doctors were still intent on their work in the ward, she skipped quickly along the corridor.

Slensky had stopped outside the office door and he looked to make sure there was no one watching. The coast was clear, so he nipped inside and across the room to the desk. It as the work of a moment to slip the desk drawer open, grab the key, and carefully close the drawer again.

He was round the desk and back to the door in a moment. He called softly to Margaret Conrad.

"No one coming, is there, Miss?"

"Nom of course not." Margaret frowned with irritation. ""Why all the fuss? He is only a patient, after all."

"Yes, Miss, of course, Miss, but you ain't seen Dr. Stein in one of his moods like I 'ave. I'm doin' a big thing for you, Miss."

He nipped quickly round the door. Although she realized it was far below her dignity, Margaret found his nervousness catching. She trotted on tip-toe behind him until they were round the corner out of sight and climbing the rickety wooden staircase to the attic.

Margaret looked at the crumbling wall-plaster and the paper hanging by its corners. Each step creaked as she put her weight on it, and that peculiar, dry, musty smell that attics have, assailed her nostrils. What a place to keep a patient! But then her honesty forced her to admit that by the same token, the whole of the main ward should be emptied and taken somewhere else.

She paused on the top step while Slensky inserted the key in the lock, and turned it with a grating noise that set Margaret's teeth on edge.

Impatiently she waited while Slensky slowly opened the door and then poked his head round the narrow opening and peered into the garret.

As he opened the door, Slensky's nostrils flared like a dog scenting game. This was food and drink to him, something nobody else knew about. Something that put him in a position of superiority. Not only did he know that there was something special in the attic room, but he, and he alone, knew and would have seen what it was.

If he had been honest with himself, which he never was, he would have been forced to admit the sight was much less interesting that he had hoped. The room was bare save for a truckle bed, a couple of chairs, and some drawers. It was much as you might expect for a sick man in a Poor Hospital.

He turned his attention to the bed. The figure lying in it was dozing quietly, and was like any of the other patients except that it was washed and clean-shaven and. . .Slensky's eyes fixed and he licked his lips, as he caught sight of the straps. Then he saw the scar on the head of the man in the bed. A big livid scar that ran right across the forehead and into the hair.

He sucked his breath through the gaps in his teeth.

"Cor, a man wot has had his head off, and then had to be held down with straps!" That's what he'd say. This was worth something to him. He could tell it a little bit at a time; with a little bit of embroidery it ought to keep him in wine every night at the tavern for weeks to come. Margaret who had been waiting for him to get out of the way let out an imperious: "Well?"

Slensky turned with his finger on his lips, and hoarsely whispered:

"There you are, Miss, he's asleep. Don't forget to lock the door when you're finished and let me have the key. I'll wait at the bottom of the stairs, Miss."

Not knowing quite what to expect, Margaret was a little relieved at the starkness of the garret. It was much the same as the rest of the place. The plaster was cracked and peeling, but at least the room was clean, which was more than could be said for the ward below.

She slowly and quietly closed the door behind her. Somewhat diffidently she approached the bed, and the figure which was sleeping restlessly in it. She stood looking down at the man.

As she stood looking down at the head, tossing slowly from side to side, the eyes suddenly snapped open. They looked empty, then the figure gave a sudden heave as though to straighten up and the eyes gained a focus on her staring fixedly at her.

Oh, I'm sorry. Did I wake you up? she said, feeling a little foolish.

The eyes looked her slowly over. Then, in a curiously soft voice, which pronounced the words slowly and carefully, the man in the bed greeted her:

"Why, Miss Conrad, it's you!"

Margaret could make nothing of this, and only looked puzzled. The voice continued:

"Did Dr. Stein send you to see me?" This at least she could answer.

"No. I just came to see how you were."

"Thank you."

They lapsed into a silence during which the man in the bed seemed content to explore her face with his eyes. She shifted uncomfortably.

"Is there anything I can do for you? Let me smooth your pillow.

She leaned forward, raised his head and shook out the pillow. This was something she would not have done in the wards, but this patient seemed very clean and not particularly frightening, although, obviously, he had suffered a terrible wound to his head.

"You're very kind," he was murmuring.

"What is your name?" asked Margaret.

"Everyone calls me Karl."

"Are you well cared-for here, Karl?"

There was a pause before he answered:

"Oh . . . yes."

Margaret drew one of the chairs toward the side of the bed.

"I will sit with you for a little while, then you must get some sleep."

Karl nodded.

"What is your work?" she said brightly.

"I have no work."

"You will soon get some; you will soon forget about this illness.

Karl looked at her, wondering. At least part of Frankenstein's promise had been made good. His body must be normal, since this girl was sitting close to him without any real sign of the disgust that would flicker in people's eyes before Frankenstein had done his work.

"I will help you when you are better; you must come and see me . . .I will write down my address for you."

She wrote it on a piece of paper, and, since there was no bed-table, she looked round to see where she could put it.

She saw the suit hanging on the wall. She held the paper poised in her hand.

"I will put it here, in the pocket at the top."

As she did this she noticed, for the first time, the straps which were holding Karl into the bed.

Karl felt her eyes on these things which kept him prisoner. Through the gossamer happiness of having this thing of beauty talking to him without embarrassment, there shot an idea of hard reality. He controlled his voice carefully to softness.

"These straps—they hurt."

She came over, instantly solicitous, and felt them. She looked a little shocked.

"But they are much too tight. I'll loosen them for you."

The straps over his body were nothing. If she would only loosen the straps which held his wrists to the sides of the bed, he could be free. He could not expect that even *she* would be foolish enough to take them off altogether, but if they were loose, he would manage the rest.

"I will loosen them for you."

The scent of her hair as she bent over him made him feel dizzy. He closed his eyes.

She moved round the bed to the other side.

"There, is that enough?"

He opened his eyes to see she was looking anxiously at him.

"Perhaps just one more notch on this side?" he asked.

It would not matter if one hand was still tight so long as he could be sure of getting the other one loose. This, he felt, would be his only chance.

"It's the right one that is the trouble," he said softly.

He felt light with exultation as she loosened it one more notch. He could have slipped his hand out then and there if he had wanted.

"Thank you," he said. "Thank you."

He lay back and without making another move or a murmur, he let her go out of the door. He knew where he could find her, and now there was a more important task ahead of him. He had to make Frankenstein's plan for him an impossibility, and there was only one way to do this.

Karl lay tense in his bed, listening to the tap of her heels as she picked her way down the rickety stairs outside the door. He cared not move until he was certain that he was alone. He had long since realised he was at the top of the hospital building. He had recognised the stained overall which Frankenstein had been wearing sometimes when he came to visit him. If he was lucky, they might go away to the laboratory before they came up to see him.

First, he would get out of bed. He tugged at his wrist still held in the leather straps. For one awful moment it seemed that it might not come free. Then, scraping skin off the back of his wrist, the right hand came out of its leather thong.

He looked at it and worked the fingers. Quickly, he leaned on one side and, with his right hand, fumbled at the strap which held his other wrist to the side of the bed-rail.

Slightly out of his control the fingers plucked at the buckle of the strap and fumbled on the leather. He forced himself to be calm and to work slowly and methodically. In a few seconds, both hands were free.

He sat up in the bed massaging the wrists where the leather had held them. Then without bothering to undo the straps which were across the bed, he wriggled out from under them and out of the bedclothes.

Next instant, he was standing up on the bare boards. His body moved surprisingly easily. He was prepared to make an effort to shuffle his leg forward, and when he did it the leg swung free. So much so, that he almost over-balanced. He forced himself back to a slow pace.

First things first. He should have his body under control. He made a couple of slow, tentative steps in the one direction, and then he swung round and made two more back again. It was easy! He took a stride and then another until he was striding to and fro across the room.

He wanted to sing and shout. Suddenly he realised that he was already a little tired.

Karl examined himself. There were still the traces of the scars that he had seen while his body had been hanging in the tank, but his limbs were straight and strong.

He looked at the suit hanging on the wall and at his own form. The cloth looked clean and smooth and the tailoring good. He looked under the bed for the box in which Frankenstein had brought the clothes.

He dragged it out and lifted it on to the bed, and as he opened the lid, he chuckled to himself. Ah! The meticulous Dr. Stein, the all-clever, all-remembering Baron von Frankenstein. The man whose passion for detail could tell him the exact number of stitches he had put in a wound, weeks before.

If Dr. Frankenstein was buying a suit, it would be unthinkable that he should forget all the accessories that went with it. There in the box, as Karl had expected, was the shirt, the socks, the shoes—even the cravat.

Oh yes, if Dr. Frankenstein was going to put his specimen on show, nothing would be forgotten.

Karl shook out the shirt and slipped it over his head. The fresh, starched linen felt hard to his touch. He took the trousers from the hanger and slid his long legs into them. A grin of pleasure crossed his face as he realised how well they fitted.

He must look. A mirror, there must be a mirror. It was by the head of the bed. How could he have missed it, as he walked up and down?

Karl made a start towards it, and then, felt heavy with fear. Suppose that what he might see in the mirror would be something that would shatter his hopes of a new life?

Slowly, he made his way in front of the fateful piece of glass, hardly daring to turn his eyes to it. The image was blurred so he stepped forward and wiped at the grime with his sleeve, and then looked and looked.

He flexed his arms, bobbed up and down, admiring his movements. He went close to the mirror and looked into the face that was reflected back at him.

It was a lean face. It was pale. It was not necessarily a particularly distinguished face, but the eyes in it were bright, and gave it a sort of life.

He leaned closer to the mirror. There was one big blemish. Across the whole of the forehead ran a livid scar. Even as he ran his finger along it the memory of the pain came back to him. There had been times when he thought he could not endure it. He looked from his face to the other scars round the wrists, and on his chest.

He was satisfied. In time, the scar on his forehead would fade from its present livid, ridged red. It would probably always be there, but it was a small price to pay for a new life.

A new Life! His face crumbled into a mask of fury as he remembered. A new life, yes, as a medical curiosity! The attic became a cage to him. He leapt to the door tugging at the handle, and only just in time did he save himself from beating on the panels and roaring for his release.

He returned and sat on the bed, shaken by his own outburst.

"I must be careful. I must think before I do anything." Even as he told himself this, the gorge rose in him and he cried and beat his hands together. "I must get out, out . . out!"

With an unnatural clam he crossed to the attic window, opened it and looked out. Below the window was a straight drop to the ground. A drop big enough to kill him instantly if he fell.

He pushed his head out of the window and twisted round. The roof was only a few inches above the window. From there, he could find another way down.

His foot was already on the window-sill when he checked himself and dropped back into the room. The cardboard box was still on the bed, and the jacket of the suit was still on the hanger.

If he were going to walk through the streets of Karlsbruck, he would rouse considerable comment if he were to do it with bare feet and wearing nothing but a shirt and trousers. And, if the good Baron Frankenstein should have taken the trouble to have Karl's clothes made to measure, why should not he take advantage of the fact?

He put on the socks and shoes and the waistcoat. The jacket he held over his arm for he would need his shoulders free if he were to climb his way on to the roof.

At the window, he leaned out and tossed the coat the short distance to the roof. Then he stood on the sill and not daring to look down, he tried to ease himself on to the roof. His fingers dug into the moss-grown gutter. He put his weight on it and there was an ominous tearing as it moved away from the wall.

Sweat trickled into his eyes. He was almost ready to return inside the room, when he realised that by wedging the window open, he could use it as a step to raise himself up without putting too much weight on the gutter.

A moment or two of anxiety and he was on the roof clinging to the uneven tiles. He wedged his feet into the gutter and, with his hands free, he put on the jacket. Since he was leaning slightly backwards, he felt himself safe enough to look down into the yard.

On the cobbles below he could see the pony and trap that Frankenstein used to travel out to the laboratory; even as he looked at it, the figures of the two doctors came out of the building and climbed into the carriage.

He knew they must have some special reason for their journey, for them to go so early. It meant he might have trouble, when he too reached the laboratory, but at least he was secure in the knowledge that he would not be missed for some hours yet. In those few hours he could lose himself in the city.

The trap jogged out through the double gates, and Karl began his half crawl, half scramble over the tiles of the roof. He headed towards the back of the building. Over there was a kitchen and a laundry, which were in out-houses projecting some way from the building. If he could find a way down on to those, he could drop without difficulty to the ground.

Eventually, he found what he was looking for: a drainpipe that led down to the eaves of the washhouse roof. It was rusted thin, it was old, and it might come away from the wall, but if he fell the distance to the roof would be short enough to break his fall. If he rolled off to the ground he might still be lucky to survive.

Clutching the pipe, he lowered himself inch by inch over the edge of the roof until he was forced to trust his whole weight to the pipe. Then he edged down, thanking the skill of the workmen who had set the pipe so surely in its position.

It seemed hours before his feet touched the roof of the washhouse. He slid his way down to the gutter and there, in full view of anyone who came along to draw water from the yard pump, he was forced to rest.

His heart was pounding uncomfortably and his mouth was dry. Worst of all, his legs and arms ached so that they trembled beyond his control.

He decided to take a chance.

Karl dangled the long legs of his new body over the guttering, and pushed off. He landed with an awkward jar.

His hands were red with the rust from the pipe, his clothes were grey with the dust. But now that the doctors were gone nobody knew his identity. He had as much right as anybody to be in the hospital yard, and nobody would question his presence after one look at the scar on his forehead.

He peeled off his jacket and hung it on the side of the pump, rolled up his sleeves and, pushing the pump handle a couple of times, he sluiced the cold, refreshing water over his face. He drank thirstily of the water from his cupped hands and, after drying his hands on the back of his shirt, set about knocking some of the worst of the grime from the roof out of his clothes.

He lingered as long as he dared in a quiet corner of the yard and then, unobtrusively, slipped out through the double gates.

Karl had made the journey to and from the laboratory to the Poor Hospital so many times for Frankenstein, that he knew every alley and every short cut on the route.

If there was a dark way, he took it. Once or twice, lone strangers whom he passed, turned and watched his lean form as it walked unsteadily in the direction of the city gate.

It was not merely the scar on his head which made them turn, but the look of fire in the eyes which seemed as though they belonged to another person, who was propelling the lank form along by sheer force of will.

They little realised how near they were to the truth. Karl's every limb was aching with the fatigue from the unaccustomed effort. He was not really recovered, and it was small wonder that his walk was unsteady. However, most of those that he passed, put the unsteadiness down to another, and more common, cause.

Darkness had fallen by the time he was near to the edge of the city and he dared to walk on the main roads, hurrying toward his goal by the shortest routes.

By the city gate he turned into the familiar weed-grown yard. In the corner of the yard by the cellar steps the doctor's trap was standing.

The horse idly struck at the flints with its hind leg and whinnied as he passed it. He drew into the shadows and waited. No one came.

The long flights to the cellar lay before him. If he were caught on them there would be no place for him to hide.

Stepping softly and bracing himself against the walls, he crept down. The door at the foot was open and the light spilled out in a shaft.

He crept to the door and then jumped across the shaft of light.

Inside, the laboratory door was open and he could hear the voices of the two doctors, slightly raised. He strained his ears to hear, but he dared not enter. He sank into the shadow and waited, glad of the opportunity to catch his breath. The doctors continued talking.

CHAPTER SIX

INSIDE the laboratory, the two doctors were doing the routine chores that had been Karl's. Frankenstein, in his black working coat, was walking along the line of cages where the animals were kept; opening each cage quickly and pushing inside the portion of food. He was talking and a little irritated.

"I really don't see what all the fuss is about, Hans. We knew that it would take time for Karl's new brain to take complete control. We must expect that it will not have complete control all the time."

He popped some greenery into a rabbit cage.

". . . and you must admit that these parozysms have become less and less frequent, particularly since the pain has died away.

Hans Kleve was standing at the end of the row of cages with his hands thrust deep into his overall pockets.

"Yes, but the brain has already control. He can speak almost perfectly and you could hardly find a more complex action for him to do than that; but still he flares up in a moment. All one has to do is oppose him or delay him something that he wants. I am worried."

Frankenstein reached the end of the line of cages and clicked the last door shut.

"Well, I am not," he said.

"Then what about Otto here," Hans jerked his head at the cage where the monkey was sitting happily scratching himself. "Well, what about Otto?"

"You said he killed his wife."

"So he did."

"Could the same thing happen to Karl?"

Frankenstein put down the empty feed boxes.

"There is no fear of that, so long as his brain is given enough time to heal. Otto was an accident; he became agitated after the operation and fractured one of the cells in his brain."

"Does Karl know what happened about Otto?"

"Of course he does and it's just as well. Karl is intelligent and as he knows what could happen to him, he will take no unnecessary risks."

Frankenstein picked up a towel and, wiping his hands, he leaned against the bench and watched the younger man pacing.

"We know that there is a risk in all this. It is always possible that the subject might, so to speak, slip down a grade in life because only the main centres, the animal centres, might join up, but since Karl can speak we know that we are past that hazard. Are you satisfied, Hans? What worries me much more is that the reactions of his right hand do not match his left; they are good but not good enough. But that is enough of Karl."

He eased himself up and crossed to the far bench. On it lay a long figure covered by a sheet.

"Hans, I want you to see this."

Hans followed, and Frankenstein lifted a corner of the sheet.

"What do you think of it, eh? It is the face that I am particularly proud of."

Hans looked at the face on the body, and then at Frankenstein, then at the body again. Once more he looked back at the face of Frankenstein.

"It's amazing," he said, "fantastic. How did you manage it?"

"I thought you would be interested. I thought there might be a time when it could come in useful. Now that it is assembled, you must give me a hand to put it into the tank."

There was no great problem of weight in lifting the body from the operating table into the tank. Frankenstein had long before rigged up a system of pulleys for the purpose.

One lowered it while the other carefully steadied it.

As it sank below the surface of the liquid, Frankenstein pointed through the glass of the tank.

"Do you remember the arm from the pickpocket? Well, this fellow in the tank is going to be the first man ever to be born with a tattooed arm."

Hans looked at the arm. There it was in place, still with its intricate spiral of twisted snakes winding up to the elbow.

"Come along," said Frankenstein. "We must get back to the hospital. Now that we have fed the animals, we had better go and feed the man who is supposed to feed the animals."

As they emerged through the laboratory door a figure squeezed itself into the deepest shadows and froze into stillness like an animal in the forest.

Frankenstein locked the door and put the key in its customary place. Their cloaks brushed the brickwork as they ascended the stairs.

As the sound of the horse's shoes clipping across the courtyard died away the figure of Karl detached itself from the shadows. He waited listening for the trap to reach the street and then he moved swiftly to the laboratory door. He reached on to the ledge at the side and brought down the key.

The lock turned without difficulty, for it was new and he, himself, had always oiled it. Not waiting to close the door behind him, he moved swiftly into the laboratory and across to the benches at the far side.

In the alcove devoted to specimens there was on the bench a lumpy shape covered by the usual sheet.

He hurried over to it and pulled back the sheet.

There lay his old body.

Carefully preserved with all its blemishes, the twisted right hand and leg, the hunch and the half-blind eye. In addition the top of the head was open and empty like the shell of a split coconut.

This was what he had come for. What he had risked his neck over. He put his hands under the armpits and pulled the body off the bench.

Dragging it behind him, Karl edged backwards to the nearer of the two big furnace doors. Supporting the upper end of his old body in his arms he hooked the furnace door open with his foot.

Heedless of the scorching heat that come through the open door he half dragged, half pushed his old body into the leaping flames of the furnace.

He kicked the door shut. The sweat from heat and effort was pouring down his face.

In the corner, in its usual place, was his own truckle bed next to Otto's cage. He gratefully sank on to the blankets. Otto seemed to know him, for he jumped up and down excitedly, seeming to recognise him as a fellow sufferer.

Karl looked at him with a crooked smile and shrugged his shoulders. "Yes, only you and I really know, don't we, Otto, and it is easier for you. So long as someone gives you your regular meals, you don't mind being on show in a cage.

Karl sighed, and studied the floor. What now? Whatever happened to him next, he could never be the freak put up for show beside his own body. There had been no conditions when he had snatched Frankenstein away from the scaffold. He felt Frankenstein was deceiving him by trying to impose them now. But could he do without Frankenstein? He had watched the progress of so many of these operations from the time they were started on frogs and lizards, not to know that until the healing was complete there must be clinical care.

He gave a snort; he himself had burned enough of the remains of the failures in the same huge furnace that was, even now, consuming his own original, twisted body.

Suddenly Karl stiffened. There was a sound outside the laboratory door, a shuffling and a clinking of bottles. Karl looked round for a place to hide, and ducked behind the tank containing the freshly made body.

The shuffling stopped, and he could hear the heavy breathing. It was Kloster, the janitor, half drunk as usual. Karl bit his knuckles. Oh God, why had he been in such a hurry as to leave the door open? If he had only remembered to shut the door that drunken fool would never have known he was in the laboratory at all.

"Where are yer?" The voice was coarse and heavy like its owner. It grated on his nerves. Otto, the chimp, set up a screaming chatter in his cage at the sound of the presence of one of his enemies.

"Shut up, you heathen bastard." Kloster's heavy form clumped across the room to the monkey's cage.

He leaned drunkenly against the cage with his fingers round the bars. Inside the cage was Otto's territory and Otto knew it. Otto jumped from his perch, seized one of the fingers, and bit it.

The janitor swayed back with a howl of pain.

"You would, would you!"

He lumbered to where the fire irons for the furnace lay. He picked out a long poker with an end that had been melted to a point.

His bestial face showed every bit of the enjoyment he was going to feel when he speared the body of the little monkey through the safety of the bars.

It was only when Kloster started to push the poker through the bars that Karl from his place behind the tank realised just what Kloster was intending.

Otto had been his friend and he could not see him done to death. The gorilla-like janitor was taken by surprise. Karl leapt out, pulled the iron from Kloster's grasp and threw it across the room.

"Kloster, you must not do that. I have told you before to leave Otto alone."

The heavy janitor looked glazedly at him.

"A prowler! I knew there was someone around. Been listening so you knew my name? Well, I'll help you remember it."

His great hand clutched one of the laboratory high stools and he raised it up above his shoulders.

Karl was for one instant frozen, then he realised the terrible danger he was in and rushed out of reach to the other side of the work-bench.

Kloster's pig-like eyes glowed a little and he swung the stool back to hurl it at Karl. One his toes Karl was wavering, not knowing which way to run, to the left or the right. He realised that the stool would come crashing at him, so he seized a heavy jar of spirit and flung it at the janitor. It shattered with a glancing blow on the stool and deflected Kloster's aim enough for the stool to splinter on the bench.

Karl tried to run for the door but in spite of his bulk the janitor was quick enough to catch Karl's coat and haul him back.

Karl felt himself shaken like a doll, the heavy wine-laden breath puffed sickeningly into his face. A little spray of spittle covered him, as Kloster panted with the effort of lifting him off the floor.

Karl was hurled backwards against the wall. His shoulder hit, and then an exquisite agony shot through him as his head struck against the hard plaster.

He slid to the floor, a ring of golden pain around his skull where the scar stood livid.

"You mustn't hit me. Please, you must not hit me."

Karl pleaded from the floor, too dazed to stand.

Kloster was beginning to enjoy himself. He liked 'em when they cringed.

"No, I won't hit you," he grunted as he leaned down and hauled Karl to his feet.

"Not hard, I won't," and with that he crashed the back of his hand across the side of Karl's head with every ounce of his strength.

Karl went skeetering across the laboratory into one of the workbenches, where a shower of retorts and bottles was shaken down.

Kloster moved towards him, enjoying himself hugely.

"Now, I'll have to hit you for all the damage you just done." He guffawed at his own joke.

For Karl, the world had stopped. He was not on earth nor in heaven; he was in one big cloud of pain. There was a screeching noise and he couldn't tell whether it came from inside his head or whether he had made it with his mouth.

His eyes raised from the belly to the coarse face above, with its broken nose and broken teeth.

Karl's body felt strangely light as he clambered to his feet. His body was steel, his body was hate. His civilization fell from his like a cloak.

"Aaaarrh!"

The throat of his enemy. This was the throat of his enemy between his hands. This was the throat where his fingers were sunk deep. This was his enemy, his enemy, his enemy.

The blows that were rained on Karl's face and head were as nothing. His fingers like steel claws bit deeper and deeper into the janitor's throat.

The throat and the man began to sink before him and twist and convulse. And then it was quieter and still. There was no more danger.

Karl's fingers and wrists ached. He relaxed them to him; once more he had a body.

The mists that had blurred his vision were clearing, leaving him with a terrible exhaustion. He leaned back on his heals, panting.

"Chirrrrk-chirrrrk."

The sound came from a cage by his side. Of course, it was Otto. He stood up. What was that at his feet? He looked down at the lumpy form with its head sticking at an awkward angle like a chicken on the butcher's bench.

There was a fractional stirring of the hair on Karl's neck. The enemy.

He gradually began to piece together what had happened, and what he had done.

He buried his face in his hands to shut out the sight. All his life he had wanted to love and be loved by people, and now that he had the form to be like them, he had killed.

Allow, it was a man whom he had always detested, but he had killed.

One thought dominated him: he must get away. Away from this staring fact of his . . . he was struck cold with the thought.

His madness? He must have help. Who could he turn to? If he waited for Frankenstein to return, the cold eyes would bare at him. He knew he was an experiment that had failed, and the fate of the experiments that failed was destruction. He himself had carried it out often enough; the injection from the poison bottle and then the furnace.

There must be someone. Someone who wanted nothing from him and was willing to give. A recollection jutted through the haze in his mind, and feverishly he scrabbled in the pockets of his coat.

From the pocket he drew the folded slip of paper which had been given him by Margaret Conrad. Her address; she would find a way. She would give him rest.

He read the few lines on the paper and, stuffing it back in his pocket, he fled out of the spirit-smelling room and up the stairs out into the night.

He was heedless of whether people saw him or not. If they were frightened by him he didn't notice or care. Through the darkened streets he hurried, past the edge of the market, into the town centre, and out up the hills toward the big luxurious residences of the rich.

The air was cold, and as he walked his brain became clearer. He slackened his pace to a more ordinary speed. He stripped off the cravat and threw it away, and kept to the shadows when there were people passing him.

He turned into the coach roads of the district where they built no pavement, because it was never considered that anyone would walk along the roads. The only ones to use them would ride in carriages and those who could not, did not matter enough to warrant a footpath.

Once or twice on his way through the elegantly laid-out parkland he took shelter in the bushes at the side of the drive as a carriage with its lamps flickering, rolled past him carrying the homeward-bound guests from the houses.

Eagerly, he read the names on the big double gates until he found the ones which he sought. It was normally a peaceful world, the world of the high society that lived around Karlsbruck. The gates were not locked.

Pray heaven they kept no dogs at the house of the Countess Barcynska. Once inside the gates, he glided into the shadows at the side of the drive and padded softly along on the grass.

Even as he came insight of the big house he could see the lights being extinguished one by one. With long strides he loped across the lawns toward the front of the house.

He passed some children's play-things; a wooden horse, a tiny wheelbarrow; and then he was at the edge of the drive.

The gravel crunched with a sound that almost echoed in its loudness. Karl hastily stepped back on the lawn.

It would be impossible for him to ring at the door. With the condition of his clothes and the bruises on his head, they would as like as not give him a penny piece for a loaf and slam the door in his face. He would have to find Margaret Conrad in person.

With infinite care, he crept across the drive to the house and edged his way along to the nearest lighted window. It was a lobby, and it was empty. He moved to the next and through it he could see people at the far end of the room.

Bending double he slipped past window after window until he was close to them. His anxious eyes scanned the group. There was an old man who looked only at a book and there was Margaret Conrad. They were all laughing together and talking across an old man whose head was buried in his book. It was hard to tell whether he was asleep or reading.

"Dear girls, at this time tomorrow the affair will be in full swing." The Countess Barcynska gestured with the little cup of chocolate that was precariously balanced in one hand.

"After the string concert, the orchestra will be over there for the dancing session, and, my dear Margaret, don't think that we in Karlsbruck cannot compete with the salons in the capital . . . !"

Karl listened as the old woman chattered on and on. Then, as she had finished her chocolate, she slapped her hand with her fan and ordered the girls to bed.

"I want you both rested and looking your best. Now off with you! And none of this sneaking down to the stables to look at the foal."

"Oh, Auntie Barcynska, you are mean! Why not? Can't we say goodnight?"

"No! If you want to see that confounded little beast you can get up early and do it in the morning. Now be off to your rooms."

The Countess leaned over to the old man and prodded him with her fan. "We are going to bed, Grandfather," she bellowed at him. The old man nodded vaguely at her and retired into his book.

Karl backed away from the window watching the progress of the girls by the light of the candlesticks they were carrying.

He walked round the corner of the house watching the candles travel along the corridor.

There was a balcony outside Margaret Conrad's room, but there was no way up to it that he could see. He doubted that she would come if he were to call; and if she saw him as no more than a vague, shadowy figure, she would be too frightened to talk to him.

He remembered the talk in the salon. She was going to the stables in the morning. If it was early, there would be a chance that she might be alone. But though he realised he would have to wait till morning, his eyes watched hungrily at her room

After ten minutes, her windows were opened and she stepped out on to the balcony. Karl's mouth was dry. He felt he had never seen anything so beautiful. Her dark hair had been loosened from its slides and flowed over her shoulders. Oblivious of the watcher below, she stretched herself and every line of her body showed through the thin shift.

Then she dropped her arms and, as though she could see the tall thin form in the shadows which was watching her, she crossed her hands over her breasts and disappeared inside the room. A second later the light went out.

Karl stood with his knees trembling still watching upward, trying to convince himself that she would appear again.

Then the cold struck through him. He would need to shelter. The stables were behind him. The lock gave him little trouble; it was no more than a big old-fashioned catch.

Worried that he might disturb the horses so that a groom would come to quiet them, he stood for minutes inside the door, not daring to move. Finally, he edged his way along to where the foal was tethered.

The box by the side was used only for straw. He stepped into the box and he had barely time to cover himself with straw before exhaustion swamped him, and he slept.

At the hospital, Frankenstein and Kleve climbed the stairs to the attic. With the little tray of food in one hand, Kleve inserted the key in the lock with the other.

"I am willing to bet that he is still sane," said Frankenstein. "Come on, open the door."

Kleve pushed the door open. For an instant he stood stock still, then rushed into the room, the light flickering in the lamp which he carried. Frankenstein followed him in and unceremoniously dropped the tray on one of the chairs.

"But . . . he was asleep when I left him, I gave him the sedative," Hans Kleve stuttered.

Frankenstein examined the empty bed and carefully looked at the straps and the window wedged open. It was obvious by which route he had gone. Frankenstein was angry and puzzled. But why? Controlling himself, he spoke to Hans:

"What happened before you gave him the sedative?" he asked coldly. His self-control burst and he shouted at Kleve.

"Pull yourself together, man . . . tell me . . . there must have been some reason for him to do this."

"I . . . talked to him as you said I should. He asked about his future."

Fury settled over Frankenstein's face.

"You told him that?" He slapped Kleve's face, almost beside himself with rage.

"You stupid fool. You told him that. Have you learned nothing of human reactions?"

Frankenstein gradually managed to force control back on himself. He broke away from Kleve and marched back and forth across the room, rhythmically beating his hands together and muttering to himself.

"Let me think, let me think . . . where would he go? Ha!

Suddenly he stopped his pacing.

"The laboratory," he cried, and rushed down the rickety stairs followed by a penitent Kleve.

The two ran past the office and out into the yard leaving a rather surprised Slensky, holding the two grogs that he had just mixed for them. He heard the trap start off. As it ran out of the gate, he shrugged his shoulders and drank the grog first from one glass and then, contently, he drank the other. Those two were mad. Nobody but a madman would order him to get two hot grogs and then run away into the cold night without drinking them.

Kleve and Frankenstein both lived with their individual apprehension of what they might find when they reached the laboratory, but neither of them had bargained for what they did find.

The place stank of the fumes from broken spirit and ether bottles, and all over the floor there was a mess of broken retorts. In the centre of the mess lay the body of the janitor.

"Of course, the janitor would think he was an intruder." Frankenstein looked round at the extent of the damage. "Suppose his brain was damaged in the fight?"

Frankenstein walked round the littered benches to the specimen department, and from there he went to the furnace and opened the door. He looked in. Shielding his face, he picked up an object from the edge of the fire with a pair of tongs.

"Hans, come here and look at this." He held out on the end of the tongs a charred, half burned and twisted boot from which protruded the bones of a foot. "See, he came to destroy his old body. That is his right foot; see the twist in it?"

He tossed the morbid relic back into the flames.

Then, wiping his hands and almost to himself, he murmured:

"He knows he will need my help, he knows that. . . ."

He jerked himself back to hard reality. "This janitor will have to go into the furnace. You must give me a hand."

The two of them struggled to push the ancient foe through the furnace door. Finally, perspiring slightly, they rested.

"You must go back to the hospital, Hans; I shall wait here. I do not know how long it will be, but some time he must seek us out, and we should be easy for him to find."

As Hans Kleve went through the door for the yard, Frankenstein put on his old black working coat and began to clear up the mess that littered the laboratory.

The man had caused them this upheaval slept, quietly and deeply, in a stall of straw at the stables of the Countess Barcynska.

Jimmy Sangster

CHAPTER SEVEN

DAYLIGHT was filtering through the windows of the stables of the Countess Barcynska, and as the patch of sunlight from the window moved down over the wall it caught the figure bundled in the straw.

Karl became conscious of the light in his eyes. He roused himself. He had dreamed he was once more a hunchback, that Frankenstein had bent over him with a needle in his hand saying, "You are a failure, Karl, and you know what we do with the failures, don't you?"

Karl jerked into wakefulness, but it was a minute or two before he could remember precisely where he was and why he was there.

His head ached and his eyes were twitching. He sat up in the straw to massage his hands, which were numb from resting his head on them.

He stretched his legs out and made to stand up, but his right leg would not answer to him. His face went grey as he looked at his foot. The right foot was turning in, the way it had turned in and twisted on his old body. The body he had dared to risk life itself to lose.

His face twisted tight with agony of mind, and he allowed tears of self-pity to roll down his cheeks.

He rubbed at this left hand to bring the circulation back and though the flesh was pink, in his mind already it seemed to be twisting round into the useless claw that had been his before he won his new body.

He sat in the straw rocking himself in silent misery. He must have help before this went too far. If they could work on it now, Frankenstein and Kleve could help him. But Frankenstein was a perfectionist. It was perfection or nothing.

There was a rumbling of bolts, and the light came flooding into the stables as the doors were opened.

Karl peeped out from his hiding place and watched the figure of Margaret Conrad walking toward him. The light from the doorway behind her formed a glossy halo on her hair. She stopped in front of the foal's box.

"How's my darling?"

The foal turned round to her unsteadily and gazed back with big, dark eyes.

The foal remembered a friend, and with jerkly half-controlled movements stepped over to nuzzle Margaret's face.

"How's my beauty, eh?"

"Miss Conrad . . . Miss Conrad?"

Margaret raised her head from butting at the foal's neck. Someone was calling her name, and it was not in the country burr of the coachman, Josef.

"Miss Conrad."

She looked in the direction of the voice, then caught her breath.

Standing in the straw on the other side of the low barrier into the next box was a haggard man. Had it not been for the beseeching look in his eyes, she would have run in fear. Then she saw the huge livid scar across his forehead and remembered the patient of Dr. Stein. The special patient in the attic room. Her eyes widened in surprise.

"What are you doing here?" she asked, with one arm still round the neck of the foal.

"I had to get away . . ." With a desperate movement Karl waved the piece of paper on which she had written her address.

"You said you would help me."

The man was obviously distraught. That he meant her no harm, she was sure.

"Does Dr. Stein know you have left the hospital?"

For a second, the man's eyes showed fear. He put out his hand as to protect himself and, frantically, the words tumbled out. "No, don't tell him, please don't tell him!"

Margaret made up her mind she must get help to him.

"It's Karl, isn't it?" He nodded his head eagerly.

Karl clung to the wooden pillar that rose up by the box. He clung to it rather like a child that is afraid of being taken into a dark room.

"Let me stay here."

"But you need to be looked after; I must tell Dr. Stein."

His voice rose to a shout.

"No!"

Margaret frowned. It was clear that whatever had happened, Karl was becoming a little unhinged. She would have to be tactful.

"But Karl, you can't stay here like this."

"You are a kind lady; please, not Dr. Stein." The voice had dropped back to its normal soft tone. "Not Dr. Stein; the other one."

"Dr. Kleve? If I promise not to tell Dr. Stein and to get Dr. Kleve, will you stay here until I get back?"

Karl nodded eagerly.

"All right then, I won't be long, and you must wait."

Now that he was sure of the course of events, Karl's figure relaxed so far that he almost crumbled against the wooden post that he had been holding with such nervous strength.

Margaret went to the stable door and called the groom.

"Josef, there is a man in the fodder stall by the foal. He is from the hospital; he is ill. I have to fetch the doctor, so I want you to get me the trap ready. When you have done that, I want you to look after him and bring him some food."

Josef touched his forehead.

"Yes, Miss Margaret."

Margaret Conrad ran off toward the big house and the groom wandered down to the box to see this stranger that Miss Margaret had picked up.

Josef could not honestly say that he liked what he saw. However, Miss Margaret's orders were to be obeyed, and if a girl like her was not afraid of this man then there was no reason why he should be.

"There is a pump in the yard," said Josef. "You'll have to wait for the rest until I've harnessed up for Miss Margaret."

Karl nodded, and said hesitantly in those peculiar soft tone of his: "Thank you" but would not move until Josef had turned on his heel and gone to see to the horses. When he was at a safe distance, Karl emerged and, limping slightly, picked up a bucket and filled it at the pump.

The cold water helped to calm his feelings, and he became acutely aware of the hunger gripping his stomach. It was nearly a whole day since he had eaten.

But like an animal, he wanted to return to his lair and lick his wounds.

This was not only Frankenstein's failure, it was his own failure as well. Unless help could be brought to him soon enough.

He sank again into the heap of straw.

He watched the morning world of the big house come to life. The work-a-day world to which he yearned to belong.

One of the girls came toward the stables with a tray of bowls and a big pitcher. Josef, who had been hissing as he brushed down the horse, met her and drew her aide. Karl could hear Josef's voice in a low rumble, a moment's silence, and then the girl's giggle and she ran back across the yard.

A minute later, Josef came down to him carrying one of the bowls and the pitcher. It was hot gruel, and the pitcher contained fresh milk. Josef handed it to Karl without a word, and Karl suddenly found himself wolfing the contents of the bowl.

Josef stayed watching him.

"Hurt your head?"

Karl nodded without lowering the bowl from his mouth.

"I . . . it was an accident."

"Who's the doctor?"

"Dr. Kleve."

Josef hitched himself away from the edge of the stall where he had been leaning, and spat idly.

"You ought to see Dr. Stein; he's the clever one; all the toffs go to see him now."

He left Karl still wolfing at the bowl.

With the food in his body, Karl began to feel the life beginning to flow in him again. He dragged an upturned bucket to where, although he was hidden from the outside world, he could sit in the sun and watch the yard.

As he watched, Margaret Conrad came round the side of the house buttoning her gloves and dressed in a morning coat that glowed away from her as she walked.

She walked over to the stable door. Still buttoning her gloves, she poked her head inside.

"Karl? Oh, there you are. Don't forget, you promised to stay here till I come back."

Awkwardly Karl pulled himself to his feet.

"Yes, Miss Conrad."

Margaret turned to Josef, who was holding the head of the chestnut.

"Josef, you will keep an eye on him."

The younger of the coachmen was holding the door of the carriage open, Margaret taking his hand to climb in. The footman folded the steps, closed the door and ran round to leap lightly into his place in front. He picked up his reins and the landau jerked away down the drive.

Margaret Conrad gazed over her shoulder at the stable door.

What was it about this man? When he looked at her his eyes burned and he looked at her as if he was hungry. Yes, hungry. Margaret felt herself reddening. She leaned forward.

"Boris, can't you get to the hospital a little more quickly?" she said sharply.

The coachman cracked his whip and sent the horses to as fast a trot as he dared.

The landau rattled into the edge of the town and Boris was forced to rein down slightly as people were going about their daily business. They clopped through the market area and out to the big house where Doctor Kleve had his private surgery.

Boris drew up, and opened the door for Margaret. Margaret stepped to the pavement and ran across up the stairs to the surgery.

She waited impatiently for the answer to her tug on the bell pull. An old, bent housekeeper opened the door. Margaret stepped inside.

"I want to see Dr. Kleve, please."

"He don't work here now, Miss. He moved his surgery over to Dr. Stein's."

"Is he over there now?"

"No, Miss."

Margaret was beginning to snap a little at the old woman's obtuseness. "Well, where is Dr. Kleve now?"

Finally, she managed to get the answer that she wanted.

"You'll find him over at the Poor Hospital at this time, Miss."

Margaret ran down the steps and climbed into her landau.

The long-spoked wheels of the landau glittered as Boris finally drove through the dilapidated gates of the Poor Hospital.

In the hallway, Slensky was leaning as usual on his broom when Margaret came running in through the front doors.

"Morning, Miss; you're nice an' early today."

Margaret paused. "Where is Dr. Kleve?"

"I think he's up in the office, Miss, doin' the out-patients."

Margaret was about to rush straight on, then thought better of it and returned slowly to Slensky.

"And what about Dr. Stein; is he here this morning?"

Slensky settled his chin comfortably onto his hands on the top of the broom handle. He gave a now sort of leer.

"As a matter of fac', Miss, he ain't been in yet this morning."

Margaret could read what was in his mind, as if it were an open book. "Disgusting man." she thought, but she didn't have time to bother about him. She turned and gathered up her skirts to run up the stairs to the office.

Hans Kleve was to preoccupied pinning the last of a bandage into place to look up as she entered.

"Rest the arm as much as you can," he was saying.

"Hans, I must speak to you. It's urgent."

Hans looked up and saw her, and gave her a nod to indicate he had heard, but continued talking to the patient. He patted the bandage on the woman's arm.

"That's fine now," he said. "Come and see me again in about three days."

The moment the patient was outside, she closed the office door, and with her hand still on the door knob she turned and faced Hans Kleve.

"I found Karl this morning. He's in the stables at my aunt's home."

"What?" I must get Dr. Stein."

He had already taken one big stride to reach his hat and cloak when Margaret's voice cut in on him.

"No."

Hans Kleve stopped.

"No, Karl is terrified of him. He seems to think that Dr. Stein will kill him."

"But that's . . ."

"Please! The poor man is nearly out of his mind. I promised I wouldn't bring Dr. Stein, and I won't break my promise."

Hans considered for a moment. He knew a little of the obstinacy that Margaret Conrad could produce. If he tried to get Dr. Stein she might, in her ignorance, try to seek help from one of the other doctors in the town, and that would be a catastrophe. He took down his hat and picked up his bag.

"Very well. I had better come myself."

Margaret whirled and pulled the door open.

"I have a carriage waiting downstairs."

The carriage swung out through the suburbs to the green of the big park, Hans and Margaret sitting in it side by side. Little by little the story of how she had loosened his straps had come out, then they each sat silent, each with their own doubts.

"He said he was in pain . . . and I thought I was helping him," said Margaret in self-reproach.

There was no blame that Hans could make. If he had not spoken so loosely, Karl would never have thought of running away.

"Of course you did," then he leaned forward. "Can't you go faster man?" to the coachman.

They ran through the gates and on Hans' shouted instruction, Boris, the coachman, took the carriage round to the stables instead of the front of the house.

Josef came forward to hold the lathering horse.

Hans and Margaret ran into the stables and towards the hay stall. Margaret call as the ran:

"Karl! Karl! I've brought Dr. Kleve."

There was no answer; the stall was empty.

Margaret stopped dead, and Hans came up to her and looked over her shoulder. Margaret turned a worried head to him.

"But he was here! I left one of the grooms to look after him. . . . Josef, where are you?"

Hans moved to the stall and gloomily looked about.

The indentation in the straw, where Karl had slept the night, was clear, but there was no sign of Karl. Josef, the groom, came in, leading the sweating horse that had brought them out to the Countess' home.

"Josef. Where's the man I told you to look after?"

"I dunno, Miss. I went for some water for the horses and when I came back he was gone."

Hans returned from poking around the corners in the stable.

"Dr. Stein will have to be told now," he said.

"Shall I come with you?" asked Margaret.

"No, you stay in the house. I must go back to town and tell Dr. Stein."

"You had better have the carriage. Josef can harness a fresh horse for you."

Josef touched his forehead and bellowed to one of the stable boys to see about the fresh horse, then he went to the little harness room at the end of the stable for his cocked hat and his coat. There was something in the wind and he wasn't going to miss it. He would take the Doctor back to town himself.

Hans paced up and down, tight-lipped, while the fresh horse was being brought. What had caused Karl to go off again without warning? This was becoming dangerous. Karl was not only dangerous to himself but to other people. Heaven knows what might happen if someonc saw him and jeered at him.

Hans was worried by these journeyings. It was a long way from the Countess Barcynska's house to the town. By the time he had got back to town and found Frankenstein it would be well into the afternoon, and it could be dusk before he and Frankenstein could return to the park. To hunt for Karl after dark would be an absolutely hopeless task.

He wedged himself into the seat in the carriage and they set off, bucketing along the road and out to the old city gate where the laboratory was situated.

When they reached it, some prudence bade Hans to tell Josef the coachman to stop outside the old brewery, and not to take him inside the yard to the actual entrance to the laboratory.

"Wait here for me, Josef," he said, "and be ready to go straight back to the park again."

Hans disappeared down the alley on the next block; to the warehouse and then, when he was out of sight, cut across the yard. Frankenstein was sitting in the laboratory with the door open. The operating couch was laid ready and Frankenstein was gazing up at the new body that hung in the tank. He looked at Hans as he came in, dust-covered from the drive.

"Well?"

"Karl has been out at the Countess Barcynska's house. I went to see him but he had gone."

Frankenstein shot to his feet.

"Why didn't you tell me? Where is he now?"

"I don't know. He must be somewhere in the park."

"We must get out there right away. We must find him before anyone else does.

Frankenstein grabbed his cloak from the hook and crammed his hat on his head.

"These ignorant fools may get frightened by his looks and kill him——" He paused for a moment. "——or be killed by him. Have you a carriage?"

Hans nodded. They left the laboratory, but in spite of the rush Frankenstein halted at the door, and looked round to see that everything was in order before he shut the door, carefully turning the key in the lock.

Josef had already turned the carriage and was waiting, talking quietly to the horse while he held its head.

It was one of the most uncomfortable journeys Hans had ever made. Apart from the bucketing about of the fast-running coach over the bumpy roads, there was the tense silence that Frankenstein kept until they were almost at the park. Then impatiently he asked: "How much further is it?"

Hans looked out. "This is the park now. The countess's house is on the other side."

"Can't we go any faster?" called Frankenstein. Josef on his box cracked his whip and called to the horse, but they were travelling nearly as fast as he dared. By now it was dusk, and the road through the park was an ornamental one which twisted and turned through the woods to give the best view rather than the quickest route.

As he came round one of the bends, ahead of them in the road was a group of people with lights. On the road, a red light was being waved for them to pull up. Josef stamped on his brake and reined the horse in. The sparks fell in a shower from the rim of the wheel as the brakes bit in. He pulled the coach to a stop just by the group with the lamps.

"Why are we stopping?" asked Frankenstein.

A uniformed man detached himself from the group and walked over to where the carriage had been stopped. Frankenstein recognised him as the senior police inspector of the district. The man saluted.

"Oh, it's you, Dr. Stein. Sorry sir, but we have to check everybody passing this way."

"What's the trouble?"

"Murder, sir."

The two doctors flicked a glance at each other. They opened the door of the carriage and stepped down with a nonchalance that neither of them felt. They had to know. Was it Karl? Or was it Karl's work?

Frankenstein flicked his gloves on the palm of his hand.

"This is Dr. Kleve. Perhaps we could be of assistance to you. You know—the cause of death and so forth."

"That's very good of you, Doctor. It is over here."

"When did all this happen?"

"About an hour ago. But we are sure the man is still in the area, and we have a full description of him. Here it is sir." The inspector lifted back the sheet from the head of the body that lay on the bench.

Frankenstein kept his features under a rigid control for what he might see. He looked down. It was the body of a girl. It was not Karl. The head of the body lay at an unnatural, grotesque angle as had been the head of Kloster the laboratory janitor.

His worst fears were confirmed, but Frankenstein made a pretence of an examination. He rose and pulled on his gloves.

"There is not much doubt about the cause. You say the man was seen?"

"Yes, the boy who was waiting for her saw him—that is, if it was a man. He didn't walk like a man but went like a spider, and there was a great big red ring round its head, with blood pouring out of it. Sounds fantastic, doesn't it sir. But then," he indicated the body with his head, "it was no ordinary murder, as you have seen for yourself."

The two doctors climbed into the carriage.

"Drive on, Josef," said Frankenstein, "but now please go slowly." Then in an undertone to Hans he said: "You look out one side, I'll keep a watch out the other.

The carriage rolled slowly along the winding drive and the two men peered out on either side.

"It's no good," said Frankenstein, leaning back into the carriage. "Even if he were there, he would probably stay away from the road. We had better go and talk to that girl Margaret Conrad. There may be something that he said to her which will tell us where to look. And we *must* find him." He looked sharply at Hans. "You realise that?"

"Of course we must," said Kleve. "He is a danger to everybody, running round the way he is."

Frankenstein permitted himself a grim smile as he looked at the eager profile of his assistant.

"My good Hans," said Frankenstein, "perhaps I pushed you too far ahead too quickly with this work. We live still surrounded by superstition and prejudice. You must realise that Karl is not only a danger to himself, he is a great danger to us. To you and me."

"We cannot hide the killing . . . we can only hide the killer." He sat inscrutable, and after a long pause he added ". . . if we can find him."

The thin carriage wheels crunched on the gravel as they turned up the drive to the House of Barcynska.

CHAPTER EIGHT

WHEN Karl watched Margaret Conrad's carriage drive off, he felt, for the first time, that he was becoming the master of his own destiny. True, he had come to ask aid, but it had been aid on his terms, and it seemed as though she was prepared to abide by those terms.

Anyone, but not Dr. Stein.

He dragged his upturned bucket to where the sun was striking warm through the stable doors and he sat on its hard wood boards. He leaned against the door post. The air was full of the heady scent of morning. The moist earth was giving up its richness and mixing with the perfume of the flowers that skirted the yard. The very essence of life itself was flowing round the garden.

Josef the coachman passed him on his way back to the kitchen with the empty pitcher, and Karl watched the leathery figure with its bowed horseman's legs clumping toward the big house. Karl sighed. There was a man with no problems.

Karl watched as Josef returned from the kitchen and with him came one of the maids. The girl was skipping along nervously, and as she came closer, it was obvious that she was deliberately trying not to look at Karl. Josef and the girl came over to the door of the stable and Josef turned to the girl.

"Wait here, I'll get it for you," he said, and disappeared inside the stables. The girl stood twisting her skirt to and fro so that on each twist she could take another glimpse of Karl. At first he had been watching the sway of the girl's lithe body, but he knew this pattern too well; he felt a hot flush mounting his face.

Josef came out again with the brush which had been the excuse for her to come. He held it out to her.

"Here you are."

The girl gave a high-pitched giggle.

"Thanks, Mr. Josef," and sneaking one last look at Karl, she ran back to the house with the brush in her hand. Josef busied himself very deeply with his duties so that he could not catch Karl's eye.

After a short interval, another one of the maids came out from the kitchen bringing the brush back.

Karl felt his heart begin to pound. The anger tightened in a band round his forehead and the scar began to burn.

The girl came towards him and darted as many glances as she dared when she passed him to go inside the stables.

"Here is your brush back, Mr. Josef," she said in an unnaturally loud voice.

As she went, she cast a sly sideways glance at Karl, and then with another smothered giggle, she fled back to the big house to spread her gossip about the stranger.

To Karl, it was as though a knife had been twisted in his vitals. The agonies he had lived through strapped in the bed in the attic at the Poor Hospital, and for what? To be stared at by giggling serving wenches?

He stood up with a jerk that sent the wooden bucket on which he had been sitting rolling into the gutter. He looked for Josef. The man was at the far end of the building, drawing water.

For a second Karl was impelled to go after the man and turn his complacent face to one of fear. Then mastering himself, he looked for a place to hide. He knew that he must see Kleve; he knew that he must wait but he could stand no more staring eyes.

He wrenched himself away from the doorway and, with a speed that surprised himself, he strode across the yard and into the shrubs, caring not that he crushed his way over a bed of flowers and broke the small branches of the shrubs.

He walked and walked, and then he ran, an awkward loping gait. The very effort of his movements was a lotion to the pains in his mind and his heart. He ran, and as he ran he cursed.

There had always been dreams. Dreams of life with a straight body. Now that dream was coming true, but it was no longer a dream but a nightmare.

He found himself at a stream and there he dropped exhausted. He leaned against the bole of a tree and buried his face in his hands.

Slowly, through his fingers, tears trickled down his cheeks. He remained silent and the tears still ran. Every now and then, a harsh sob racked his frame. Between the sobs he was so silent, so taut, that he hardly breathed.

Such a pain of mind could not last, and the hell in his mind be came an oblivion, through which he drifted into sleep.

He woke stiff and cold on the ground. He rolled over, for the time forgetful of what had brought him where he was. By his head was the withered stump of a tree draped with climbing plants. A bee solemnly droned away from it, laden heavy.

Karl sat up, and to him came a return of the bitter memories of that day. Numbed, he sunk his head in his hands.

"What's the matter, mister?"

Karl stiffened at the sound of the thin, young voice.

"Does your head hurt?"

Karl looked up and saw regarding him solemnly, the ragged figure of a small, dark-haired girl. She wore the full-patterned skirt and the black-velvet jacket of a gypsy, and in her ears were heavy, gold rings.

She was squatting on her haunches a few feet away from him, a chain of flowers swinging in her fingers. She was entirely unafraid.

"If your head hurts, you ought to see my granny."

A bitter-sweet smile twisted Karl's face, he shook his head.

"When grandpa's been out of a night and in the morning his head hurts, granny boils some herbs and gives them to him to drink, and he is all right again."

Karl struggled to his feet, his head throbbing with a band of pain round it. The girl, still squatting on her haunches, watched him.

"Mister, you look sick; come on, it's only a little way." She got to her feet and tossed her ring of flowers on to the water of the stream. "I'll show you."

Karl rubbed at the stiffness of his face where the tears had dried, and moved after the child as she picked her way along, skipping over tree roots and ducking under branches. In a minute Karl could smell the smoke of a wood fire, and hear the sounds of voices. Instinctively, he slowed down against the thought of meeting again with humans.

The girl looked round.

"It's only the family." she said, and then a little magnanimously, "you'll be all right if you are with me.

She marched on ahead of him, and Karl followed numbly.

The clearing was by the edge of the stream and in it were three caravans. Gaudy colours chased round their woodwork. The horses were hobbled and were idly chomping grass from the edge of the clearing.

A cooking fire was glowing under the iron pots that were hung over it. Women were tending the fire and shooing off hordes of children. The children were all dark, with big black eyes. Their clothing diminished with their age, until the youngest, barely able to toddle, were tottering around quite naked.

Karl's guide made her way to the biggest of the caravans. On the step there sat an old crone puffing at a blackened pip with a silver band on its stem.

"Hey, granny! I got a man with a scar. His head hurts."

The girl was obviously a favourite child. She clambered on the steps of the caravan and sat down on the step below the old woman. The woman stroked the head of the girl and looked at Karl, who had stopped in the centre of the clearing on the other side of the fire.

The girl twisted her head to look at the old woman.

"He's got a scar and it's better than Uncle Peto's she said triumphantly. The old woman took her pipe from her mouth.

"Come here to me, man. We do you no harm if you come as a friend.

Karl walked round the edge of the fire, watched curiously by the younger women.

The old woman was a queen and her eyes were bright with intelligence. The skin of her face was wrinkled into hundreds of creases, the deepest of these running down from the sides of her big hooked nose.

"The child says you have a pain."

Karl nodded.

"Aiee," she breathed. "It's a fine scar! It could bring gold pieces if you want to beg with it, but this is the work of one beyond our skills.

"I can ease this for you, but only one who can care for you properly, is the one who gave you that scar.

The old drone broke into Romany and chattered a few words to the girl at her knee. The child ran into the caravan and soon came back with two earthenware jars. The old woman called for hot water from the cooking pot, and then with her gnarled fingers, she rubbed some of the herbs from each jar until they were little more than powder.

"Hold your hand out, man she told him and shook the little heap of powder on to his palm. "Put that on your tongue and then swallow it with the water." She handed him a scoop of hot water.

Karl tilted the powders into his mouth and washed them down with the water. The left behind a slightly bitter taste where grains of them stuck to his teeth.

Even as he took a second mouthful of the water, his head lightened, and the pressure round his skull was eased.

"How came you to get this scar, young man? Come look into my eyes, and tell me."

Karl looked at the old woman's face, and felt that for her there was nothing less than the truth.

"I am seeking a new life in a new body," he said simply. The old woman put her pipe back into her mouth and sucked it.

"Get an ember for my pipe, child," she said, without taking her gaze from Karl's eyes.

The child returned with the glowing stick of wood and the old woman sucked at her pipe until the blue smoke was flowing easily out of it.

"Why should you seek a new body?" Once more Karl felt that there was no room for anything but the truth.

"My other body was ugly and twisted. I was lame, far worse than now."

Still keeping her eyes on him the old woman put out her bent fingers and said.

"Give me your hand, stranger."

Karl put out his left hand.

"And the other."

He pushed forward the one which had been paralysed. The old woman studied them carefully and turned them over and back again.

"Tonina," she said to the child, "look well into the hands and remember them." Then she pushed Karl's hands back gently to him. Her old husky voice questioned him once more.

"And with your new body, what is you wish?"

"Old woman, I wish to dance and be gay with people."

"Man, you shall be gay and dance to-day, with us; would that please you? But on one condition. Before the dusk you must away and seek the one whose work is on your head."

Without waiting for his answer, she clapped her hands for attention and rolled out rapid Romany to the members of the family round her. Some of them looked a little strangely at Karl, but the old woman's word was law, and from the caravans were brought the guitars and the fiddles. Before long there was a wild music in the air.

With the music came the wine. It was passed round in leather bottles which each person held up and poured into his mouth without touching the lip of the flask. The bottle came to Karl, and he drank.

He watched the dancers whirling and jumping in front of him and as the wine bottles emptied he found himself clapping in time to the music. The dancers were swinging round in a circle, and at a sign from the old woman, two of the girls broke away from the circle and came to drag Karl into the ring. He hung back.

"Go on; dance man," said the old woman, nudging him with her pipe. "To-day you shall dance as you never have before, and you never will gain."

Karl allowed himself to be pulled into the circle and he danced. He was clumsy, he was slow, and the others laughed, but he didn't care, because they were laughing with him and not at him. There was a break and, exhausted, he came back to the old woman on the steps.

She called a girl who brought him over a flask. He held it up away from his face as he had seen the others do, and the wine splashed over him as he drank. The music started again and he was dragged off to dance. The wine was making him bolder and he flung himself into it with all the energy he possessed. When the music stopped he returned to the caravan steps with his arm round the girl who had been dancing with him. She was laughing as she held up the leather bottle for him to drink again.

The old woman pointed at the sky. "If you must be at the big house by dusk you must leave us now," she said. "Remember you must go to see the only one who can help you."

Karl looked at the sky and at the trees. He was lost. He laughed about it.

"Mother," he said, "I will do as you say, but which way?" The old woman pointed with her pipe. She had an arm round the child who had brought him.

"You will come to a road; it leads you all the way."

The wine fumes clouded the pain in his head, and he was happy. He bowed to the old woman, and to the child.

"Good-bye, mother; good-bye little one."

He swung round, and unsteadily he made his way into the trees. As he went, the music started up again behind him.

The girl looked up at the beaked face of the old queen.

"I shall remember the eyes and the hands, grandmother, but why?"

The old woman hugged her close as the two of them watched the figure of Karl disappearing in the trees. Then she took her pipe from her mouth.

"Because, child, that is the face and the hands of death."

Karl blundered his way on toward the road. He was flushed and hot. Every now and then he would pause while the streak of pain rounded his head. Then, as it subsided, he would plod on his way, his senses in a blur from the wine and the old woman's potion.

He walked with a limp, but he was only partly aware of it. It gave him a peculiar sidling motion which looked the stranger for the speed at which he was moving.

Sometimes he would brush against a tree to solid to give way, and he was staggered slightly off his chosen path. It was not long before he came to the carriage road. The shade of the trees was ended and he stood swaying in the late afternoon sun.

A carriage rolled past him, the harness jingling, the two footmen sitting upright on their box.

Karl watched it pass. His eyes followed the figure sitting in the back lolling easily against the padded leather.

Karl spat after the wheels of the carriage in his hate for the world he had never been able to enter. He shouted after the retreating carriage.

"There's nothing you can do that I can't."

The effort of shouting caused a pain to shoot round his scalp. He had to have rest. He needed treatment. They should give him treatment. They had used him for their experiments and it was up to them to make things good for him. So the girls from the kitchen had giggled at him. So what were they? Nothing. Coarse, thick, heavy girls. Hadn't he, Karl, that very afternoon danced with his arms round the waist of a lithe Gypsy girl, with flashing eyes and teeth that gleamed when she laughed? Kitchen maids, pah! It would be Countesses for him.

He set off on the road muttering to himself, and watching for another carriage to come, so that he could spit at it. On the road he stumbled. The loose flints thrown to the edge of the drive made him unsteady, so he clambered back on the verge. He was able to move faster over the beautiful, spongy green. Roads were made by men.

He spat; what did he want with roads? Grass was from God for other gods. Only fools rattled and rolled along in boxes hung from wheels.

He stopped short as another agonizing stab of pain rent through his head. He gritted his teeth and clenched his fingers, not daring to move until it had faced.

Ornamental paths were tracing their way in and out of the woods and clumps of oriental bushes had been planted here and there as cover for dalliance, where Karl cut away from the winding road to make his way through the bushes.

As was his custom, he was sliding along on the grass verge, his footsteps making no noise. So it was that he came upon the girl,

She was young and she was pleasing to him. Her hair was caught up behind her ears and hung in glittering ringlets almost to her shoulders. She wore a blouse of the thinnest muslin and, through it, Karl could see the swell of her young breasts. Below, the corselet of her bodice pulled tight round a waist so thin he could have put his hands and touched his fingers at either side.

She was a girl waiting for a man. And was not he a man?

Karl stepped off the grass and in front of her.

He bowed unsteadily.

"Madam, I am he for whom you wait."

The girl drew back from him, but behind her was a bench and above, on the other side, a terrace.

"I have danced the whole afternoon," he said. "You, too, should dance today." His arm slid round her waist and the feel of her body under his hand made him giddier than the wine had done. He leaned over her.

Her hand swung the little ornamental bag at his head. As it touched, his brain exploded in a golden pain that forced his hands to grip tighter still. The muslin tore under his grip. Out of the haze, another explosion of pain ringed his head.

The boy was still hurrying on his was across the park to his rendezvous, when in the distance he heard the screams. He stopped. There was something about them.

The boy broke into a run, a fear in his heart. He pounded towards the far-off sounds, but long before he had reached them they had died, and he could see a flock of birds circling, too frightened to return to their nests.

"Marie! Marie!" The boy ran on, calling her name. He came to the place of their rendezvous. She was not there. He called her name again. Then on the ground by the stone bench he saw the little vanity bag. The strap was broken and the contents spilled.

Heading away from the path was a trail of broken bushes, and, here and there, on the twigs were little scraps of torn muslin. He ran down this trail, shouting her name again and again.

It was under the beech tree that he saw the tatters of the pretty flowered dress, and the gaunt grey figure that rose up from it like a thin human hook. The figure was bent in a stoop, the hands were shaped in claws, and round its head was a vivid red band that dripped crimson.

The boy hurled himself forward.

Karl saw him coming and through a cloud of pain and fear he fled into the undergrowth. He crashed on until the pain in his leg forced him to slow down. He looked round. He was alone; the boy had stayed behind. Karl could no longer stand upright. His eyelid was drooping grotesquely. Only his hand remained still unaffected.

Karl knew that unless he had help he was reaching the end. He would rest, and then he would make his way back to the big house. They had promised him help. If he could reach it, the damage might still be undone.

The sun was dipping slowly, too slowly; he could wait no longer. Clutching at the nearest branches he hauled himself to his feet. He must find the road again.

Karl clawed his way on.

He stopped. Straining his ears, he held himself taut. Over the rushing noise in his ears he could hear the sound of voices. With infinite care he stole forward. He could see the glimmer of lanterns in the dusk.

It was the place.

A flash of memory flooded into his mind and he shut it off for fear he would scream at the horror of it. He worked his way carefully round the group with their lamps and their uniforms, and his heart leapt.

He had found the road.

He was about to step on to it, when he heard a carriage running along the flints. He stepped into the shadows and watched as the carriage was halted by one of the uniformed men.

The passengers alighted and stood talking by the side of the carriage. In the glow of the carriage lights, he recognised Stein, the two men he most needed in the whole world, Frankenstein and Kleve.

They moved into the group around the figure. He dared not move toward the halted coach for fear that someone might see him. He waited. When they moved off he would catch them.

After a while they came out and got into the coach, which started to roll slowly towards him. He was about to leap into the road, but watching the carriage move away was the figure of the man in uniform.

The carriage came opposite to Karl and he could see that Frankenstein was peering out into the dark woods.

Karl looked back. The man in uniform was still standing in the roadway. The carriage was passing and Karl dared not shout. It was moving slowly, and Karl dragged himself along the bank trying to keep up with it until they should be far enough away for him to shout or throw himself into the road.

But with each painful step that he took, the carriage drew a few paces further away from him. It was going so slowly a child could have run to catch it.

But Karl was lame.

Once again he was a lame Karl who could only drag one foot. A few more paces and they would be out of sight from the group on the bend.

The, as he slithered down the bank into the road, the coachman whipped up the horse and in a moment the carriage was beyond his call. Karl fell against the verge and sobbed.

He would follow. Dragging behind the world, as he had always dragged behind.

The sound of a carriage on the road once more drove him to scramble up the verge into the grass and the bushes. He waited until it was safely out of sight and dragged himself on, too weary to drop on the road.

The lights of the big house twinkled at him. He forsook the edge of the driveway and slipped into the sweet-scented bushes that ran along the side of the lawn and round to the kitchen garden.

Opposite the kitchen garden was the stables. That would be the first place they would look for him.

He came to the edge of the kitchen garden and stole round the rough brick wall until he was at the edge of the stables.

Inching his head forward he peered into the stable yard. It was full. of carriages. Grooms were flinging blankets over the horses, and fastening on the feed-bags.

From the stable came the sound of men's laughter. There were oil lamps turned up high. Creeping round to the side of the building he raised himself enough to see into the stable. The grooms and the coachmen were sitting around; the cards were out.

It was impossible for him to get into the stables unnoticed. Then he caught sight of something which was out of place in a stables. Two tall, silk hats moving along the other side of one of the partitions. One disappeared for a while as the wearer bent down. They were in the fodder stall.

The hats came into view again, and the figures moved into the alley way and out of the entrance.

The two men were Frankenstein and Kleve.

Karl padded to the edge of the wall and hissed desperately to attract their attention as they came out of the door. They neither turned nor stopped. They walked directly away from him toward the big house. Karl leaned his hot, aching forehead against the cold corner stones to keep himself in control.

CHAPTER NINE

IT had completely escaped Frankenstein's mind that he had ever been invited to the Countess Barcynska's musical evening, so used was he to refusing such invitations.

The two doctors picked their way in between the empty carriages waiting at the sides of the drive and round into the kitchen yard. The lights inside the stables were bright and there was a crowd of footmen and grooms around the door.

"It will be practically hopeless with all that crowd around," said Frankenstein, "but at least we can look. It is possible that he hid himself inside there in the hay loft, and now he dare not show his face for all the people that have arrived."

As he looked into the stall Frankenstein realised the heaps of straw were deep enough to cover a man. He poked with his stick, then looking over his shoulder at the men in the far end of the stable, he bent down and called softly:

"Karl. Are you there, Karl? There is no one near to the stall. You can show yourself."

"It was too much to hope." said Frankenstein. "He must be around outside."

Despondently, he stood with his head down, thinking, and all the time flicking at the straw with his stick. He jerked round to Hans.

"I must see that Conrad girl."

The two men turned and walked slowly out of the stable, unaware of the eyes that had watched them, and unhearing of the voice that whispered after them.

Karl watched them walking across the square yard on their way back to the big house.

He dragged himself away from the side of the stable and worked his way round from the edge of the yard toward the kitchen. Each time he passed the back of one of the waiting carriages the horse in the shafts would stamp its feet restlessly, and bring on itself the curses of the stable-lads, who had been forced to stay out in the yard to keep an eye on them.

Karl reached the kitchen, and here he paused. Here there were more lights and more people. The place was humming with activity.

As he watched, the kitchen doors were open and from out of the scullery came hurrying the scullery maids, all with pails in their hands, which they brought over to the pump outside the kitchen door. They began to pump and the call:

"Christian, hey Christian! Come on out and do your work, you lazy dog."

A voice like an alpenhorn answered them from within, and a moment later the kitchen doorway was filled by a man with a frame to match his voice. He stood there guffawing at the crowd of maids round the pump.

"You weaklings! So you want me to come and do your work for you. All right, I will." He came lumbering down the steps. He slapped a couple of the maids on the behind as he came to the pump.

"I'll do it, but you'll pay for it."

He was a giant of a man, and he rolled up his sleeve and took hold of the pump handle. He worked it up and down till a steady stream of water gushed out faster than the girls could fill their buckets. He rocked with laughter at their efforts to avoid getting wet, and they squealed in mock distress as the water splashed on to their feet.

One by one the girls trooped back with full buckets and once again Christian was left alone by the pump.

Grumbling good humouredly he moved up the steps and into the kitchen.

It was Karl's opportunity. For a moment the yard was empty, and until the girls had poured out their buckets there was a good chance that nobody would come out of the kitchen door.

He dragged himself quickly across the stone-flagged space in front of the open door, and a couple of seconds later he was safely hidden in the shadows of the walls.

He had made the effort so suddenly and so hard, that he was panting, and although the sounds of the work and the chatter of the girls would have covered him, he clutched at his breath to try and silence it.

He was trembling with tension and anxiety. Help was at hand if he could only reach it. He cursed the husky Christian and his harem of scullery maids; if he had only been able to cross the yard without hindrance, he might have reached the front drive before Frankenstein and Kleve had reached the house. As it was, by the time he reached the drive, there was only the carriage of the latest arrival being led away to a place outside the stables.

Karl looked down the drive from his hiding place in the bushes. He had to be sure. He waited, facing the stables.

There was no sign of the two tall figures in their top hats and the long cloaks.

He moved to a position where he could see the portico of the main front doors. Only the two footmen stood there, pulling down their waistcoats and tugging at their white gloves, waiting for the next carriage.

He shuffled from bush to bush until he was next to the house, and peered in through the windows. There was a crowd of people, milling in the hall, but on the far side, handing over their hats and cloaks, he could see the two men. Their heads were close together and they were obviously deep in talk about matters other than the social whirl that was going on around them.

Frankenstein handed his hat to the footman and began to unhook the clasp of the silk cords on his cloak.

"I must see that girl, Hans."

He swung his cloak off his shoulders and draped it over the arm of the waiting footman. They moved slowly across the hall, peering this way and that for a sight of Margaret Conrad.

Frankenstein held Kleve's arm and pulled him back as they neared the entrance to the music room.

"Hans, we can't go in there yet. Is there no way we can find out first if the girl is inside the room?

The usher at the door was announcing the names of the guests as they entered, and as the two doctors approached, he leaned inquiringly towards them, with his eyebrows raised under his powdered wig.

"Whom shall I say, gentlemen?"

"Can you tell me, has Miss Conrad come down yet?"

The usher, who was long familiar with the fact that young men would ask specially if Miss Conrad had yet come down, permitted himself a slight smirk, which in fact he intended to be a knowing, friendly smile. He conspiratorially muttered out of the corner of his mouth:

"No, sir. The young lady is still upstairs in her room."

Kleve leaned closer to the ear of the usher.

"I don't suppose you would happen to know which is Miss Conrad's room?" he murmured quietly.

The usher pretended to look shocked.

"I couldn't tell one of the gentlemen a thing like that. . .but." a few coins changed from one hand to another.

"Well, sir, I couldn't tell anyone a thing like that, but I think that if one happened to go up the stairs and past the third door on the right, one might meet someone that they were looking for."

Kleve relaxed.

"Well, now, that is very interesting. Thank you, usher," he said, and drew Frankenstein with him to the stairs.

The usher brought his hand out from behind his back and squinted quickly down at the coins that rested in his palm.

"Thank you, too, sir," said the usher.

Frankenstein and Hans climbed the big wide staircase as unobtrusively as possible.

"My dear Hans," said Frankenstein. "I see from your enterprising little *entente* with that scoundrel on the door, that you are growing wise in the ways of the world; would that others could reach a similar state of development.

"I blame myself a lot for what has happened," said Hans, "I feel it is up to me to help as much as I can,' he paused in his sentence and added almost under his breath, "and by whatever means I can."

They mounted the curing staircase, looking neither to the right nor to the left, and Frankenstein, between his teeth, muttered:

"What this little fool of a girl did, was stupidity and interference beyond all bounds."

"It's done now. The only thing we can hope is that she can give us some clue," said Hans, as they reached the top of the stairs. The two men wheeled to the right, and as they moved along toward the corridor, Hans glanced over the balustrade into the hall. He gripped Frankenstein's elbow.

"Look down there!"

Frankenstein glanced over Hans' shoulder into the hall. By the door, and having some little difficulty about being permitted to enter was the unmistakable green-helmeted figure of a police official. The two men paused at the end of the balustrade where they were almost hidden,

A butler was hurrying forward to deal with a situation that was beyond the authority of the flunkeys on the portico.

"It's that fellow who was in the park," said Hans.

"He is the inspector. Let us thank heaven the Countess Barcynsky is a snob.

Even an inspector is going to have difficulty in getting co-operation, when the Countess has a house full of guests. But why should he be here?"

Frankenstein straightened up thoughtfully.

"That is a man of whom we must be careful, Hans. He is a plodder, but he is sound. It is up to us to keep just one jump ahead of him, all the time. If we can do that I think we shall be safe. But first the girl."

They hurried along the corridor. At the third door they stopped. Hans turned to Frankenstein.

"I think you had better let me talk to her first."

Frankenstein swallowed his annoyance.

"If Miss Conrad regards me as a bogeyman, then perhaps you are right, but for heaven's sake, let us hurry this up."

Hans Kleve knocked on the door. A voice from within, muffled by the thick panelling, called out:

"Who is it?"

Hans leaned close to the panels of the door.

"This is Dr. Kleve. I must talk to you, Miss Conrad."

The door was opened a few inches and in the opening appeared the face not of Margaret Conrad, but of Vera, the daughter of the Countess Barcynska.

"Why, Dr. Kleve . . . and Dr. Stein! Her eyes grew big. "But what are you doing up here?"

"Please, Miss Vera," said Frankenstein, "where is Miss Conrad's room? We must speak to her very urgently about one of my patients."

"This is her room, but she is dressing."

Will you please tell her we want to see her?" said Frankenstein, controlling himself. The door closed as Vera retreated into the bedroom.

Vera went skipping round the four-poster bed to the open windows that led out to the balcony.

"What are you doing out there in the cold. You must come inside. Besides, someone might see you."

Margaret Conrad came into the room, her negligee flowing out behind her.

"Margaret, who do you think is outside the door and wants you?" said Vera.

"Who?"

"Dr. Stein and Dr. Kleve. Dr. Stein said it was terribly urgent."

"It will be about that patient of theirs, but I can't talk to them up here."

Vera giggled a little.

"If Mummy ever found out she'd probably have hysterics, and make them marry us."

She got up and twirled around, watching herself in the mirror. She came to a standstill facing her reflection.

"I think I'd like that," she said and gave her shoulders a little hug.

"Oh. Vera, how can you?" said Margaret.

Well, I don't see why not," said Vera, "I think Dr. Stein is very distinguished . . . and he makes little shivers run up and down my spine when he touches me."

"I think he's horrible," said Margaret.

"You'll have to talk to them, " said Vera. "I'll help you to dress, and besides if we don't go down soon, Mama will start fussing, then we shall never get any peace all the evening."

Margaret stood up and shed her negligee.

"I suppose you are right. I ought to talk to them for the sake of that poor man. Tell them I'll see them in the ballroom."

She shivered a little.

You must be freezing," said Vera. "Look you left the window open."

She crossed the room and closed one side of the french windows that led to the balcony, but as her hand was on the knob ready to close the other window, she suddenly paused and listened.

"What's the matter, Vera?"

Vera was silent for a second and then she closed the window.

"Nothing. I thought for a moment I heard something outside."

Down below, Karl lay gasping where he had fallen, as the ivy had come away from the wall.

Fortunately, he had fallen into the soft earth of the flower bed, and he was shaken. There must be a way. But now the way was all pain. Whether he stood or sat or lay down there was pain. It was a pain that was spreading from his head down his right arm to his hand.

Minutes passed before he dragged himself to his feet. He lurched out from the cover of the house and looked up at the room with the balcony where he had seen Margaret Conrad. The light in it was dimmed.

For a while he considered the possibility of trying to climb up there again, but when he found another piece of ivy, he had not the strength left to raise himself from the ground.

He cared less and less now about the noise he might make and he sidled along by the windows to peer into the lighted rooms. One by one he looked through them, each one giving him a little cameo from life. He swayed a little as he surveyed the scene. It was crowded and there was music.

Karl knew it was Frankenstein only he must look for, and his eyes moved over the room seeking him.

Frankenstein and Kleve were in the lobby.

Hans Kleve grabbed a passing waiter and lifted two glasses of wine from the tray the man was carrying.

"Here," he said. "It may not be good manners to drink one's hostess's wine before you have been introduced to her, but I think we both need this."

The both tilted their glasses and the sharp liquor made them more alive to their surroundings.

The string quartet was still grinding away in the ballroom.

"If the young lady said she will meet us in the ballroom, I suppose we had better go there, said Frankenstein, setting down his empty glass. "Though I shudder to think what we may have to suffer."

The moved to the ballroom door, and the usher favoured them with a knowing smirk.

Hans leaned over and gave him the names. The usher, in his professional voice, called:

"Doctor Victor Stein, and Doctor Hans Kleve."

Their worst fears were realised as the Countess Barcynska caught the names and bore down on them, all billows, fan and bosom.

"Ah, Dr. Stein, so you were able to come after all!"

She extended a plump, bejeweled hand for them to kiss.

"I knew that you couldn't forget to come to our little gathering, and make the acquaintance of my daughter . . . where is she, the dear child?" Her eyes were searching anxiously round the room for the errant Vera.

"Countess," said Hans, bowing over her hand. "I believe we saw your daughter upstairs to help her cousin."

"Ah, the sweet child," said the Countess, "always helping people; but she really shouldn't have left without my permission."

"You must not blame her, Countess, it is really our fault that her cousin is late, and but for that, I am sure she would have remained by your side."

"Dear Dr. Stein, just like you to take all the responsibility; such a manly trait."

This interchange of pleasantries was becoming a bit of a strain for all of them. It was a relief when the two girls appeared in the door of the room.

"You must excuse me a moment, Countess, I have to speak to your niece." And Frankenstein brushed past the Countess before she even had time to flick her fan.

He took Margaret by the arm and pulled her to a corner.

"Miss Conrad, you must tell me about Karl. When you found him, was he the same as when he was at the hospital?"

"Yes, but he was very distressed."

"Was that the last you saw of him?"

"I think so."

Frankenstein guided her to the edge of the room and continued to fire his questions at her.

Through the window he was being watched by the man he had come to seek.

Karl straightened up from the frame and started to sidle over to the window nearest to Frankenstein and the girl. With luck it looked as though they might even come out on to the terrace. He dragged another couple of hurried steps, and then pain struck him.

It travelled down his arm from and round his head. He stopped, clutching his hand; and then before his eyes the final hell appeared.

His right arm, as though it were not part of him, slowly twisted itself up and across his body until it was once more the stiff, inverted claw, that had always been the hand of his old pain-ridden body.

It was more than Karl could stand; he had only one thought in his mind. Help. He had to have help. He stumbled over the terrace and hurled himself at the french windows.

The crashed open under his weight, and he stood swaying inside the ballroom, surrounded by a heap of broken glass.

The music died raggedly into silence.

Karl dragged himself forward towards the girl and the doctor. It seemed to him that he hurled himself onward, but in face he only dragged himself another step. He held out his paralyzed hand and into the horrified silence his voice cried out brokenly:

"Frankenstein, Frankenstein. . . . Help me!"

There was a crunch of wood and crash of broken glasses as Karl fell forward across a table, and then on to the floor, and lay still.

Kleve darted forward and knelt by his side. Frankenstein reached the fallen figure a moment later. Kleve could feel no pulse. He was about to say:

"He's dead, " but before he could finish the word Frankenstein broke in on him:

"This man is very ill. We must get him to the hospital immediately."

After the first shocked silence, the room was gradually developing a hubbub. Servants seemed to be running everywhere, and an increasing number of ladies were having hysterics.

Hans looked at Frankenstein, puzzled, and felt again for the pulse. There was nothing, no sign of a beat.

"Victor," he whispered, "Karl's dead. There is no pulse at all."

Frankenstein gave him an almost imperceptible nod and then for the benefit of the rest of the room he said:

"Please do not crowd round him. He must have air. Come Hans, help me, we must take him outside."

The two of them lifted the limp form between them, and Frankenstein called to Margaret Conrad:

"Miss Conrad, would you please call the carriage for us. We must get him away for treatment immediately."

Margaret nodded quickly, and ran ahead of them through the french windows. The two doctors reached the edge of the terrace and awkwardly backed down on to the grass verge with their hideous load. They reached the edge of the drive.

"Put him down here for the time being," gasped Frankenstein, lowering his end of the body.

"But why? Victor, why take him to the hospital?" asked Hans.

Frankenstein took him by the arm and led him quickly to the edge of the terrace. He pointed inside to where the Countess Barcynska was having hysterics, for once in her life quite genuinely; by her side was Dr. Molke and talking closely to Dr. Molke was the figure in the grey-green uniform and the *pickelhaube* helmet.

"That is why, Hans. We must prevent the authorities from finding Karl's body and identifying it." His face hardened. "More important still, we must be able to conduct a post-mortem to find out exactly what happened to Karl. Karl alive would have been of the greatest service to science. He can still be of service even though he is dead. We learn by not repeating errors.

Inside the room, Molke was enlarging to the police inspector. He would not have wished to have admitted it, but he was somewhat shaken.

"It was quite fantastic, Inspector. This, this man was in such a dreadful state, he hardly looked like a man; it was like a sort of monster. He came crashing into the room and then he stood there and called out for help, and collapsed. If a patient is dangerous he should be kept under control in the Poor Hospital, and not allowed to chase his doctor all round Karlsbruck."

At this moment the Countess came to, and sat up. She surveyed the wreckage of her musical evening, and promptly dissolved into hysterics again.

Molke was forced to transfer his attention to her and the administration of over-strong smelling-salts, in an effort to shock her back to normality.

The inspector was thinking. The description that he had just been given by Dr. Molke, fitted only too exactly the description given by the boy in the park. If the man had been a mental patient, then there was nothing to be done other than formalities. He had been taken away, and was in the charge of the two doctors, which was as it should be; and if he required it, no doubt they would produce the man for identification. If the man was sick, then he would probably never be brought to trial. The doctors would sign the necessary certificates and the formality of days in a stuffy courtroom would be unnecessary.

"I tell you, inspector," Molke's voice broke in on him. "That should never have been allowed out of a locked room. Dammit, his mind was in such a state he couldn't even get his own doctor's name right."

"Indeed, Doctor? Exactly what did this fellow say before he collapsed?" asked the inspector, who had long since lost his curiosity, but felt he ought to have a quote for his files, if one was available.

"He said, Frankenstein, Frankenstein, help me'"

At that moment neither of the men remembered the significance of that name.

The inspector awkwardly wedged his notebook, licked his pencil, and wrote the sentence.

From the terrace, Frankenstein and Kleve watched him write. They looked at each other and, both with the same thought, they turned to the drive from the stables.

They dropped attentively by the side of the body as the carriage came into view round the drive from the stables.

The carriage stopped and Margaret Conrad jumped down.

"Is there anything I can do?"

"No, thank you, Miss Conrad. We have found Karl; let us hope that we shall be able to do something for him."

Josef had jumped down from his box to give a hand with Karl, but Frankenstein waved him back.

"We can manage," he said. "I want you to take us back to the Poor Hospital as quickly as you can go."

They arranged the body on the upholstered seat and then took their place opposite.

"Please give my apologies to your aunt, Miss Conrad," called Frankenstein as the carriage moved off with a jerk and a rush into the darkness.

The two men conversed in low tones as the carriage-horse were whipped to a gallop and the carriage swung along the winding road of the park.

"I must see Karl's brain," said Frankenstein. "There should have been nothing wrong with him. I must know if it was deterioration, or damage. If it was damage, then I know that we were right. If it was deterioration, then we may have to start all over again." Then with sudden intensity he repeated himself. "It must be damage; it must be!"

"You can't find that out at the hospital. You will have to go to the laboratory."

"I know. But I only want Josef to take us to the Hospital, from there we shall have to make the journey ourselves."

This was a night when Josef felt sure of his gold pieces, and he sent the carriage rattling through the empty streets of the town. He drew the horses panting and sweating to a standstill in the drive of the Poor Hospital.

The two doctors descended and carefully carried the inert figure inside the building.

Once more Hans and Frankenstein went through the rigmarole of moving the patient for the benefit of the curious eyes that would inevitably watch their progress, and it was another hour before they were half-dragging, half carrying the inert body down the stairs by the side of the old wine-cellars. Kleve lit the lamps in the laboratory and Frankenstein insisted on setting to work immediately.

The fear that somewhere he might have made a mistake, was more than Frankenstein could stand, and the post-mortem had to be done then and there.

At about the same time that Frankenstein was beginning his work, the rotund Dr. Molke was regaling his wife with the story of the evening's happenings. He had already told her when he arrived home, he had told her again as she poured him out his warm drink, and she was hearing it all once more as he undressed and put on his nightshirt.

"Yes, dear," she said, "and then what did this dreadful man do."

"Well then, said Molke, kicking off his slippers and sliding under the bedclothes, "then the fellow crashed in through the windows and called out: 'Frankenstein, Frankenstein, help me.'" He settled himself into his side of the mattress. "Looked a bit too far gone even for any doctor to do anything for him, let alone that fool Stein."

Molke settled himself comfortably and ran through the scene in his mind once more. Fantastic figure that fellow had been, all those scars, the one round his head, the one round his wrists, it was almost as though he had been sewn together. Yes, sewn together.

Molke shot up from his pillows.

Those scars! Supposing the man had not called Stein by the wrong name? Supposing it had been the right one.

"What's the matter, dear?" asked his wife sleepily.

Molke was too busy with the thoughts that were running through his mind to answer her. Should it be the police? No, he rejected it. If he were wrong, he would bring disaster on himself, but he could raise it at the Medical Council.

Molke was sure he was right. If he had not been so sure he was right he would never have sent his cab rattling through the streets of Karlsbruck in the middle of the night to the house of the President of the Medical Council.

CHAPTER TEN

WHEN there was work to do in the laboratory, Frankenstein seemed to have an inexhaustible supply of energy. Kleve and he carried the body of Karl across the laboratory and lifted it on to the operating table.

Frankenstein stripped off his coat and set to work.

"The detail work we can do later, Hans, but I want to cover the main features of the body while we still have the time."

He paced round the table examining here and there and dictating to Kleve. Most of it was routine and he left the most important question to the end.

Then, carefully he set about making an examination of the outside of the head. Here he was so concerned that he would not rely on his observation alone.

"Here, Hans, come and look at these."

Kleve bent over the head with him and followed the pointing finger of Frankenstein over the skull and the face.

"Mark the places of the bruises," said Frankenstein. "See, these are old, they must have happened right here in this laboratory when he fought with that drunken dolt Kloster. See the two oldest, the one on his cheek and the one at the back of his head?"

Kleve looked at them. The inference was clear. If the damage inside coincided with the damage on the outside then there would be nothing to contradict the fact that if he had remained in bed, then Karl could now have been walking about normally.

Frankenstein began to put on his overall.

"I will do the rest, Hans, and we can cheek it together. Meantime can you stoke up the furnace. We are going to need it."

Tired as he was, Hans was glad to change from the effort of keeping up with Frankenstein's lightning work on the post-mortem.

He kicked open the iron doors to the furnace and, with his sleeves rolled up, he shovelled and raked until the glare from the open furnace forced him to stand back, shielding his face. Perspiration trickled off his brow, but he realized what had to be done and he was prepared to do it.

The shovel clanged on the coal heap as he threw it back in the corner.

He turned and walked down the laboratory, until he was by the section with the table where Frankenstein was at work. Hans leaned up against one of the cupboards feeling drained of his energy.

"It's ready now," he said.

Frankenstein was sitting in his shirt sleeves at the head of one of the benches. Spread in front of him was a towel on which lay a number of instruments, and a dish, containing the brain. He was probing at it delicately, and looking through a magnifying glass at what he was doing.

Hand Kleve straightened himself up and came over. Frankenstein was right. No one could have missed the damage that had taken place. If anything, the miracle was that Karl had been able to live as long as he had.

Frankenstein put down the glass and the probe and stood up. "All right, let us get rid of it."

Between them they carried the body of Karl to the furnace and crammed it inside. Hans looked round the room and went back to the operating table. From the floor he picked up the torn coat and shirt and, returning he flung them into the furnace after the body. They blazed up almost instantly into ashes.

"Shut the door, Hans."

Frankenstein stood silent for a while with his head a little bowed.

"You know, Hans, to me that is more than the remains of an experiment we are burning. We are cremating a man with courage."

He wandered over to the bench and sat against it, his arms folded over his still-white shirt.

"You and I may be in a very precarious position, but I think we are still clear. Without the body of Karl, they can prove nothing. So the girl in the park was killed by him, so he died of an infectious disease and because of that we were forced to destroy the body. If we stick to that story, there is nothing they can prove."

"You forget one thing," said Hans. "Karl called you by your right name in front of the whole room at the house."

"Still they can do nothing. Once Karl's body is destroyed there is no proof that we, or rather I, ever made it, and officially Frankenstein is dead."

Hans opened one of the cupboards and drew out from it a bottle." He wiped two of the chemical beakers and poured into each of them a measure of brandy. He pushed one into Frankenstein's hand.

"Victor, we shall have to start all over again; but can we do it here?"

"Why not?"

"Molke was there when Karl called you Frankenstein. If he could prove who you are, it would be just the chance he has been waiting for." He swallowed a gulp of the brandy and smiled wryly. "And he would have most of the Medical Council behind him; your practice didn't come out of thin air."

Frankenstein twirled the tumbler in his hands and watched the little whirlpool of amber liquid as it swilled round and round.

"There was always the chance that I might be recognised, and I have made my plans accordingly."

He emptied the glass. "Until it is certain that I am recognised, I suggest, Hans, that we carry on as before. In the morning, I shall go as usual to the surgery, and you will go as usual to the hospital. After all, we do have patients."

They pulled on their coats with the tiredness of men who have called on their last reserves.

They plodded together up the stairs from the cellar. In the yard an uncertain sun was pushing its way through the early morning mist.

Frankenstein had sufficient time for a couple of hours' sleep before his housekeeper roused him.

She set the metal can of hot water on to his wash-stand, and brought the silver coffee tray to the table by his bed.

"There's a man downstairs to see you, Doctor. I told him to wait in the porch."

"You didn't tell that to one of the patients, surely?"

She snorted indignantly.

"Of course not, Doctor. He isn't a patient, he's a policeman. He said you had something for him."

For a fraction Frankenstein's brain raced. What trick was this. Then he remembered; the death certificate he had promised in the park.

"Oh, yes, that's right, Frau Moll. There is a paper I have to sign for him. Give him a drink and say I will see him as soon as I can. Put him in the waiting room."

By the time he had dressed and tied the usual immaculate knot in his cravat, he was feeling at his best. He poked his head round the waiting-room door on his way to the consulting room. The inspector was sitting stiffly on the edge of his chair.

He rang the bell for his secretary.

"Would you show in the gentleman who is in the waiting-room?" said Frankenstein.

The secretary nodded silently. He returned, opened the door and announced:

"Inspector Eisenkalt."

Frankenstein rose from behind his desk.

"Good morning, Inspector."

The inspector took the regulations two paces inside the threshold, clicking his shiny boots together, and made a stiff bow.

"Good morning, Doctor."

"Come along, sit down by the desk," Frankenstein indicated a chair. "I suppose you want that certificate I promised you."

The inspector lowed his form on to the chair, dropping the last inch with a slight grunt. He sat rigidly upright and his helmet was clutched against his uniform. Frankenstein had to admit to a little relief. Inspectors who had the helmets tucked under one arm did not arrest people.

"Cigar, Inspector?"

The grizzled head gave a single slight shake.

"No, thank you, Doctor."

Heavens, thought Frankenstein, couldn't the man relax at all? As he wrote his report on the sheet of his headed paper he squinted at the stolid, excessive vertical figure, and then he realized. This singular lack of relaxation was due to the fact that the inspector simply could not relax; he was wearing corsets.

Frankenstein kept his face down to the paper, but he signed with a flourish.

"There you are, Inspector, I think that will cover it."

The inspector glanced quickly through the writing.

"Your permission, Doctor?"

He deposited his helmet on Frankenstein's desk. Then he folded the paper and shoved it in an inside pocket. He made no attempt to rise and go.

"This paper covers the medical causes," he said. "Our department, of course, must investigate further into how this whole affair came about."

Frankenstein tapped at the blotter with the paper-knife.

"I understand that a patient of yours," he paused for a suitably neutral phrase, "created an incident last night at the house of the Countess Barcynska."

Frankenstein remained impassive, so the inspector continued.

"Speaking confidentially, of course, Doctor, would you say that this patient of yours was quite, er, responsible for his actions?"

All Frankenstein's doubts flared into his mind. Were they trying to trap him already? Did they know about Karl? He sifted his elbows forward on the desk to give himself a little time. Karl's body had been destroyed. The could know nothing.

"Why do you wish to know this, Inspector? The affair was quite private. I shall reimburse the Countess for any damage that might accidentally have been done."

"After the death of this girl." the inspector tapped the pocket where he had placed the death certificate, "I interviewed the young man who was coming to meet her. He gave me a description of her assailant. The description coincides very closely with that of your patient."

Frankenstein leaned back, fiddling with his watch chain. He made a non-committal grunt.

"I understand that you and Dr. Kleve took this patient away to the hospital. Would it be possible for me to see him there? Perhaps I could bring the young man who saw him. It could save us a great deal of trouble. If this patient is insane, then all that is necessary is for him to be committed on two signatures; say yours and Dr. Kleve's?"

It went against the grain with Frankenstein, to say that Karl had been mad. His brain had been damaged; but that was different. He withdrew in himself and forced a suitable formula to his lips.

"The patient was certainly a very sick man, but I would not go so far as to say he was out of his mind.

The inspector's eyebrows lifted slightly.

". . . and as to seeing him, I am afraid that is impossible."

None of the muscles of the inspector's face moved, but he bristled perceptibly.

"Why not, Dr. Stein?"

"Because he's dead."

"But he was alive last night."

"He was. But much as I regret the fact, Inspector, I must point out that on occasions, patients do die, however much we may try to do for them."

The inspector flushed a little as he realised that he had put a foot wrong. "Of course, Doctor." He recovered himself.

"Well, perhaps, the young man could come along and identify the body?"

"I am afraid that also is impossible, inspector. The body has already been cremated."

"But Doctor Stein, it is most irregular for a cremation to take place before even the death has been registered."

Frankenstein gave a shrug.

"I am sorry, Inspector, but it was necessary."

The Inspector dragged his notebook out of his pocket.

"What was the treatment for?"

Frankenstein was offhand.

"Oh, I operated on his brain; he was being treated for a paralysis."

"You operated on his *brain?*" said the inspector incredulously. Frankenstein realised his slip and glossed it over. But it was too late. Somewhere deep inside the inspector's memory there had been a little click. He could not at that moment recall what it was about, but he knew there was something.

"Well no, I mean over his brain. The bone of the skull. It is nothing new."

"But why was it necessary to destroy the body?"

"He had become infected, Inspector. Once I realised what it was, I had to get rid of him as quickly as possible; even in these days, we cannot afford to leave plague-infected bodies lying around."

The inspector was about to say something then he shut his mouth with a snap. There was that 'something' nagging in the back of his memory.

"I shall have to report this, Dr. Stein; the whole procedure has been very irregular."

"Is that all, Inspector?"

The inspector tucked his book away and picked up his helmet.

"Yes, Doctor, that will be all, for the moment."

He marched toward the door, and at the regulations two paces from it, he turned and bowed.

At the hospital, the inspector found that Dr. Kleve was even more vague than Dr. Stein about the illness of this particular patient, and moreover, he was noticeably nervous about the whole affair.

The inspector plugged away.

"Dr. Kleve, this patient. Did he have a large scar running round his forehead?"

"Er, yes, Inspector, he did."

"From an operation on his brain?" said the inspector innocently.

"Why, er, yes, that's right. How did you know?"

"It was his brain, not his skull?"

Kleve sensed a trap.

"Well, of course, the wound was all in the skull, the actual brain, er, was . . . was quite sound."

"You mean he wasn't mad?"

"Well, no, not exactly. That is, he was very upset, of course, and open to infection."

The inspector gambled his whole stake.

"The plague made it necessary to destroy the body?"

He watched the young doctor fumbling and felt his gamble had been justified.

"The infection, Doctor. I suppose it meant you couldn't keep the body."

"Oh, yes, of course, inspector," said Kleve with a genuine truth. "We didn't dare keep it."

The inspector was satisfied. There was more to this than met the eye. It might be that the two doctors were trying to cover up an unfortunate mistake on their part, or it might be that 'something' which was stirring in the back of his memory.

Kleve watched the departing figure. Straight, stiff, and inflexible, it turned out of the gateway and disappeared into the morning crowd.

Kleve knew that he should have expected such a visit, but he was an inherently honest young man, and it was difficult for him to tell lies, particularly when the man who was talking to him seemed to know as much and more about the subject than he, himself.

He was more than ordinarily sharp with Slensky when he brought in a cup of coffee for him. Slensky had laid the cup down and then hovered by the desk.

"Is it true, that Dr. Stein is really Frankenstein what made the monster, and went to the gallows?"

Kleve was horrified that the rumour should have started and spread so quickly. It was almost miraculous the way Slensky seemed to get hold of gossip.

"If he went to the gallows, how could he be? Talk sense, man."

As he started for the ward, Slensky called after him.

"Three of the patients have left, Doctor . . . not stopping to be cut to pieces . . . they said."

There was an ominous rumbling in the ward as he made his round. All the fear of Frankenstein's cold incisive personality was bubbling up to the surface. In the end he made only a superficial tour and retired back to the office.

The office door opened and someone entered. He glanced up to see Margaret Conrad watching him almost curiously. Hans Kleve jumped to his feet.

"Hans," she said, 'there are the most terrible rumours going round town. What is it all about?"

Kleve sighed and sat down. Then with his hands fidgeting nervously he told her.

"Margaret, people may say what they wish, but Frankenstein is a very great man. He cares only for the knowledge which eventually will help the world. The knowledge with which he tried to benefit Karl."

Margaret shrugged her shoulders.

"And this is the end of this fantastic scheme, the death of the man he hoped to benefit?"

"To try to transform a dwarf into a normal man . . . is that so wicked, Margaret?"

Before she had time to reply there was a tap at the door and Slensky put his head in, handing Kleve an envelope.

Hans guessed what it was from the seal. He glanced at the formal phrases.

"What is it?" asked Margaret Conrad.

"It is a summons to appear before the Medical Council. I have been expecting it. I must go to Frankenstein."

Kleve came round the desk discarding his overall, slipped into his coat, and opened the door. He was not in the least surprised to see the figure of Slensky disappearing round the nearest corner.

Margaret Conrad took him in her landau to the house.

He didn't bother to ring the bell but used his own key. There was an unusual atmosphere of quiet in the hallway.

He walked over to the waiting room door and opened it.

The room was completely empty.

Hans Kleve crossed the room to the door of the consulting room. There sat Frankenstein. A solitary, lonely figure, rocking gently in the chair behind his desk.

"Hullo, Hans," he said, and relapsed back into silence.

"Victor, have you seen your waiting room?"

"Yes. Quiet isn't it, my dear fellow? Rumor travels faster in this town than I had expected."

"The whole place is simply alive with rumours. They all seem to know who you are. Victor, you must leave the country."

Frankenstein shook his head. Kleve continued.

"I have been summoned to the Medical Council. What am I to say?"

"So the Medical Council want to see you. I'll come with you. That should solve that problem."

"That would be madness . . . Let me do what I can while you move out of their reach."

"It would be madness for me to hide . . . what can they prove? Nothing . . . I'll come with you.

Frankenstein stood up behind the desk and stretched himself. "As a matter of face, since there appears to be no call for my services here, I was thinking of going for a walk anyway."

The meeting of the Medical Council was everything that Hans Kleve had feared it would be.

It was a mixture of spite, impertinent insults and leading questions. Here and there, was a vague attempt to get at facts.

Then it was Molke who put the pertinent question.

"Why did the man at the Countess Barcynska's house call you Frankenstein?"

"I haven't the slightest idea."

"You are really Frankenstein, aren't you?"

"If you mean, is my name Frankenstein, then the answer is yes."

Kleve shot a horrified glance at Frankenstein, and there was an audible murmur round the table.

"By that, I do not mean that I am the Frankenstein that was executed. As scientifically-minded men, you must admit that is a complete impossibility, but I do admit that my name was one Frankenstein."

"You admit it?"

"Why not? It is not an uncommon name in these part and we are a large family."

"If your name is Frankenstein, why do you call yourself Stein?" Molke had been caught a little off-balance by Frankenstein's easy admission of his origin.

"The name of Frankenstein was something of a handicap; so I moved, and dropped the front part of the name. Now I use just Stein."

"Then if you are known as Stein, why did the man at the house call you Frankenstein?"

"We seem to have gone the full circle, don't we, gentlemen? Because he knew me originally as Frankenstein."

"Was he a patient, or did you create him?"

"He came to me to be cured of a paralysis. I regret that I was unsuccessful in helping him."

Frankenstein was indefatigable. It was like a sort of game: one of them would throw him the ball, and he would neatly throw it back again.

It was becoming monotonous.

The President rapped his gravel on the table.

"Gentlemen, we seem to have asked all of the questions that we had decided were necessary. We are simply wasting time asking them all over again. I move that we dismiss Dr. Stein and Dr. Kleve from this session, and we can then proceed to discuss what action is to be taken with regard to them."

For once the President could give thanks for the objectivity of his colleague, Dr. Bergmann, who also was getting bored.

"Seconded," said Bergmann.

The President rather surprised himself with the success of his own actions by nodding round the table, and before anyone had a chance to protest, he dismissed Frankenstein and Kleve.

"Thank you." He nodded at the door. "That will be all."

But there was another visitor waiting to see the Medical Council. As Frankenstein and Kleve left the room and walked across the lobby talking earnestly together, the next visitor quietly faded into the doorway of another room until they had passed.

When he felt they were safely away, District Inspector Josef-Maria Eisenkalt moved inside to seek the co-operation of the Medical Council in his problems. The Medical Council seemed inclined to assist.

Two days later, across the border, the Inspector presented himself in the company of the President of the Medical Council, and backed up by Drs. Molke and Bergmann. At the rich mahogany desk of a very senior official he obtained permission to dig.

The gravestone still looked like a little forest of stubs, and the old ones still leaned cozily toward each other. But the circumstances of the opening of the grave of Baron Frankenstein were in every other respect different to the last occasion when the soil had been dumped.

There were a large number of officials present.

Two wardens were digging in the grave. At last they had reached something. They scraped the earth aside and revealed the corpse of the body-snatcher.

The President of the Council was shocked.

"Good heavens! The body is in the coffin. He couldn't have got out."

The inspector was made of sterner stuff. Bitter experience had long since taught him that when you open a grave, you do not necessarily find either what, or who, you are seeking.

"Keep on digging, let's have that coffin out here. His clipped, official tones bore authority, and the two wardens continued to uncover the coffin.

The long, wooden box was raised on to the side of the grave and the plate on the lid was there for all to see.

It still proclaimed the occupant to be Baron Frankenstein.

"All right, open it."

Two spades were thrust under the lid and once again its contents were exposed to the open. The onlookers stared down into the open box.

"A priest's hat! gasped the President.

"And a rosary," said Molke, peering over the President's shoulder.

"We were right. Frankenstein is not necessarily dead," said Bergmann.

One of the wardens pulled out the bundle of sacking by the feet of the body. He shook it and a skull rolled out on to the ground and lay grinning up at the party round the grave.

Inspector Eisenkalt replaced his helmet on his head, and turned to the doctors.

"I thank you, gentlemen, for your help. I think this is going to prove a very interesting case. Shall we return to Karlsbruck in the morning?"

CHAPTER ELEVEN

THE inspector knew only too well the sort of battle that he was going to have on his hands. He did not worry much about the position with Frankenstein; his worry was with his own departments.

He knew the sort of arguments that would be produced when he asked for a warrant for the arrest of a man who was not only officially dead, but, in fact, had been executed.

The inspector looked at the faces of the three doctors who had come with him to the exhumation.

The President was dozing, and Molke and Bergmann were arguing with each other.

As the two men argued on, he pondered on the lack of anything positive for him to go on. It began to look to the inspector as though the only thing on which he could genuinely swear out a warrant for Dr. Stein, would be for the irregular disposal of a body. Even this was liable to be complicated by the fact that the City Council had given permission for paupers' bodies to be used for schooling and research, and Dr. Stein could claim on both those grounds that his actions were perfectly legal, even if technically irregular.

The inspector pondered on the word "irregular". He decided that was his answer. If he tried to keep this on a basis of regularity then he would have very small chance of achieving anything. He would have to rely on the irregular principle; the principle of give a dog a bad name and hang him.

The inspector decided he would have to jump several steps in his reasoning when he applied for his warrant.

He would have to rely on the magistrates being too slow to catch up on him. Once Dr. Stein was safely in a cell, perhaps methods could be found of obtaining information from him.

The two doctors were still arguing with each other when the carriage arrived at Karlsbruck.

"I tell you," Molke was saying, "that fellow Stein, or Frankenstein, is nothing more than a charlatan, a dabbler."

The president awoke just in time to catch the end of the sentence. He had been very upset by the work that had been thrust upon his unwilling shoulders in the last few weeks.

"Best thing, hang the man and be done with it," he muttered, and poked his head out of the window to see where they were.

The inspector smiled quietly to himself. This was the attitude he wanted. A real feeling of antagonism all round the town, and not too much reason to back it up. Even without the bodies, there was a chance that something could be achieved if everyone had this outlook.

"Gentlemen, what do you say that we stop and have lunch before we go back to the Council rooms? I am sure you could manage the time, couldn't you?"

The others were not averse to the idea. Since many people in the town had known the nature of their errand it would be of little hurt to their vanity to be able to drop a hint here and there about what had happened.

Lunch was long, and it was convivial. The doctors were surprised by the inspector, for he seemed in no hurry to move, and once he had unbent, he had quite a fund of stories. Perhaps not quite drawing-room stories, but amusing enough.

The inspector rose from the table with the others. He saluted them with suitable respect as they climbed unsteadily into their carriage an departed.

The inspector about-faced and made his way stiffly and, unlike the doctors, steadily up the steps into the town hall. He acknowledged the heel-clicking of the uniformed porter with a nod and a wave of a finger. Salutes were reserved for those who were senior to him.

He knocked on the door of the magistrate's room. Inside the door he took his regulation two steps and saluted. Then he removed his helmet and tucked it under his arm. He stood to attention slightly to the corner of the desk, and waited to be spoken to. On an occasion like this it would never do for him to tail in the formalities. The magistrate was rustling his papers nervously.

"Eisenkalt. What's all this about a doctor who sacrificed a priest, so that he could come back from the dead? And all this business about his being able to make men commit murders just by looking at them?"

The inspector felt a quiet glow of satisfaction. He knew that the warrant for the arrest of Dr. Stein was as good as signed.

Frankenstein tired of seeing the waiting-room empty. Although he loathed to admit it, he could not work at the laboratory while there was so much to distract his mind.

There was only one place left for him to go. He went down to the Poor Hospital and tried to lose himself in work.

Hans tried to keep him away.

"Victor, there is too much feeling about you here. It would be far better if you would remain out of sight until the whole thing has blown over."

"My dear Hans, germs and disease won't wait and you have far more work here than you can cope with."

Hans opened the office door and pointed down the corridor to the surgery.

"Look at the number of people there are outside that door. A week ago they would have filled the corridor; now there are only three of them."

Hans watched him disappear into the surgery. He turned to go back inside the office to find Slensky standing behind him, watching.

"He ain't going to go round the wards, is he?" asked Slensky.

Hans nodded.

"He didn't ought to," said Slensky, "it ain't safe."

Frankenstein dealt with the three out-patients with meticulous care, taking as long as he could over each one of them. He sat for a while in the chair by the desk hoping that someone else might come along. Nobody did.

He stood up and marched off down the corridor. As he passed the office door he put his head inside and called out:

I'm going into the ward now. I'll send Slensky for you if I need help with anything."

Hans knew it was useless to try to stop him. He just sat at the desk and nodded.

The ward reeked of humanity, unwashed and festering. There was always a faint blue haze from the number of the patients who secretly or openly smoked their pipes. The sound of the conversation had an ugly edge to it. Normally the sound was thick, coarse, and jovial, but that day there was an indefinable hardness to it.

When Frankenstein entered the ward, a slight hush came over the place, but in a moment it had disappeared. The voices were raised and ugly.

Frankenstein began his round. It was the start of a battle of wills and he knew it. He casually took the first patient in his path. He picked up the chart, looked at the man and wrote a new prescription on the chart.

Once more he moved and halted by the bed. He picked the chart off the foot of the bed. A voice shouted:

"Killer! You ain't goin' to touch me!"

The barrier was broken, but it was not Frankenstein who broke it.

"You ain't a doctor!"

"You been living off of our bodies!"

"You ain't human; you been eatin' other people!"

Frankenstein flushed and stood his ground.

"Don't be ridiculous," he said. "I am a doctor and all I seek is to cure people."

He stood too long.

Someone at the back threw a bottle. It is always someone at the back.

The bottle missed him and shattered on the medicine cupboard. It seemed to act as a signal.

A crutch struck him on the shoulder. Hands grasped at him and pushed him to the centre of the ward. The men in the room were growling at him like animals.

Frankenstein tried to push his way to the door, but a blow from behind felled him to the ground. As he lay there, boots hacked at him and he was rolled in the broken glass.

Slensky watched from the corner of the ward, lacking the courage to do anything else. He darted from the ward and ran to the office.

"Dr. Kleve," he shouted. "Dr. Kleve, come quick. In the ward. They're killing him.

Hans rushed from behind the desk, sped down the corridor and burst through the double doors into the ward.

"Stop this!"

A hush fell over the ward.

The knot of patients who had been gathered round something on the floor broke up, and backed away. They were becoming conscious of a guilt for what they had been doing.

Kleve darted forward and pushed them aside.

Frankenstein lay on the floor in a pool of his own blood. His head was covered in cuts and a mass of broken bruises. He had been terribly beaten.

Hans dropped on his knees beside him. There was a pulse still flickering.

"Slensky," Hans bellowed, "get me the ambulance ready!"

"Victor, can you hear me?"

The swollen lips moved, and Hans bent close to catch the words.

"Hans. Remember always . . . this is the real enemy." The voice was barely a whisper. " . . . fear . . . born of ignorance . . ."

"Victor, you shall live. I promise you."

The breathing became shallower till it hardly existed.

Hans Kleve stood up. There was only one way, and now he was decided on it.

Frankenstein was unconscious and the pulse under Kleve's fingers told him that the life was ebbing fast.

"The ambulance is out, so I got your carriage, Dr. Kleve."

Watched by a silent ward that lacked the courage to be hostile, they carried the inert form of Frankenstein down the steps and into the carriage.

"Hold him there, Slensky, hold him tight." Kleve leaped on to the box and set the carriage rattling through the town.

He scattered the walkers and drove other carriages curing into the edge of the road.

As they reached the old district towards the gate, Hans pushed on even faster, until finally, through the city gate, he hauled on the horse and worked it to a shivering, sweating standstill.

"All right, Slensky, give him to me."

Hans took the form, and heedless of the blood that was seeping from it he held it high in his arms.

He hurried unsteadily with his burden across the yard to the laboratory.

If he was to succeed he must be quick.

At the bottom of the stairs he was forced to prop Frankenstein against the wall while he reached for the keys on the ledge over the door.

The lock turned easily and Hans with his burden, half ran to the operating tables.

Gently, he laid the form on the long bench, and leaned over it. There was life, just a little life.

He had to hurry.

He rushed across the room, stripping off his coat as he ran. He kicked the big door shut and dragged the trolley of instruments into position. He draped a sheet over Frankenstein and began his work.

He could not have told how long it was before he became aware of the thunderous banging on the door.

Quickly he pushed a jar out of sight under the bench.

Hans Kleve pushed aside the instruments he had been using. He walked slowly over to the door, wiping his hands on a towel.

There was another impatient hammering from the outside. Hans opened the door. The inspector stood there, flanked by the President of the Medical Council and Dr. Molke. Hans moved aside for them to enter.

The inspector came in first. He kept his helmet firmly on his head.

"I have a warrant for the arrest of Victor Stein."

Hans nodded.

"You had better come inside, Inspector."

The inspector and the others moved in a little procession into the laboratory.

"Where is Dr. Stein? he demanded.

Hans said nothing, but walked over to the operating table where the figure lay covered by a sheet. He lifted the sheet at the head of the bench.

The others closed round either side of him and peered at the still form which lay with staring eyes and wax-like skin.

"What happened?" said the inspector.

Hans shrugged his shoulders.

"It was the patients at the hospital . . . they went mad and practically tore him to pieces. I brought him here and operated on him in the hope of saving his life . . . we have equipment here which is more modern than anything at the hospital, but . . ."

He shrugged his shoulders again.

"I cannot work miracles."

The inspector turned to Molke and the President.

"Will you gentlemen please look at the body. I want to be sure that Dr. Stein is quite dead."

The president and Dr. Molke raised their eyebrows at the inspector.

"He could hardly be anything else, Inspector. Look at the state of his head," said Molke.

"Nevertheless, I would like an official opinion, please."

Hans was worrying. Time was against him, he must start work soon. The two doctors went through the formality of feeling for a pulse.

"He is quite dead," said Molke.

"I will make arrangements for the collection of the body and for its burial in unhallowed ground."

Hans edged toward the door, and stood at the entrance listening to their footsteps going up the stairs. When he was satisfied they had reached the top he suddenly sprang into action.

He slammed the door shut and carefully locked it. Then he set about quickly laying out more trays, and carefully selecting the instruments into groups.

Then he looked at the figure in the glass tank, the tattoo on its forearm showing clearly through the fluid. Soon it was ready in place on the table.

From under the bench where he had placed it when the inspector knocked on the door, Hans took the large jar. He placed it by the side of the operating table.

In it was the living brain of Baron Frankenstein.

Hans Kleve looked at the brain in the jar and the body from the glass tank.

"Pray heaven," he said, "that I have the skill to do this."

EPILOGUE

A DRIZZLE of mist softened the edges of the buildings. Harley Street, London, was professionally and respectably quiet.

A cab clip-clopped amiably to a stand still outside one of the tall houses, and a woman and her daughter stepped out and into the big doorway. They paused at the door and ran their finger along the little row of brass plates giving the names and qualifications of the occupants of the building.

"This is it," said the mother, and rang the bell.

Inside the building two men heard the bell ring in their office. The young one looked at the other man.

"That will be your next patient, Dr. Franks. Better clean up."

The older man nodded. He rolled up his sleeves and sent the water gushing from the taps. As he washed, he turned his head from side to side looking at the thin line of a scar which ran across his forehead.

"It is quite remarkable, Hans," he said. "You really were an excellent pupil . . . the scar hardly shows."

He shook the drops of water off his fingers and dried his hands. At the elbow of one of his arms there was another big scar, now fading with time. For a doctor, his arm was unusual.

Just below the scar, from the elbow to the wrist, there ran an intricate tattoo of twisted snakes.

OUR NEXT ATTRACTION

CPSIA information can be obtained at www.ICGtesting.com
Printed in the USA
BVOW030607240212

283719BV00006B/20/P

9 781593 933753